ON THE CULTURE OF HARMONY

On the Culture of Harmony

Where Are Human Beings Headed?

2ND EDITION

Gordon Wang

iUniverse, Inc.
Bloomington

On the Culture of Harmony
Where Are Human Beings Headed?

iUniverse books may be ordered through booksellers or by contacting:

iUniverse
1663 Liberty Drive
Bloomington, IN 47403
www.iuniverse.com
1-800-Authors (1-800-288-4677)

ISBN: 978-1-4502-9228-3 (sc)
ISBN: 978-1-4502-9230-6 (hc)
ISBN: 978-1-4502-9229-0 (e)

Library of Congress Control Number: 2011904278

Printed in the United States of America

iUniverse rev. date: 01/02/2013

CONTENTS

CHAPTER ONE

ORIGIN OF THE CULTURE OF HARMONY

Harmony as the Core Law of the Universe

The great ancient Roman philosopher Saint Augustine was well-known for saying, "The occurrence of a miracle does not violate the law of nature. It only violates the nature that we currently know."

The Culture of Harmony originated in remote antiquity. Having gone through a prolonged development process, it is now just on the upswing.

The viewpoint of the human body embryology holds that, during the process of the fertilized egg's becoming divided into body cells through mitosis, a DNA experiences a semiconservative replicating process. Therefore, a body cell has also acquired a set of genes that are the same as those of the fertilized egg. It also has potential capacity for growing into a new organism. A relatively complete and independent part of the organism is exactly an embryo containing the information of the whole organism.

Proponents of the big bang theory believe that the universe originated from a primitive atom—the cosmic egg. At one point, this cosmic egg suddenly erupted in a gigantic explosion. The material world broke the shell of the cosmic egg and came out. Thus, the universe was born. The universe has been evolving for fifteen billion years or so since its birth.

The cosmic egg contained all the information in the world as we know it today. The universe that formed during the big bang is only the manifestation and evolution of the original information. Everything in the universe is replicated and comes into being from numerous "universal hereditary genes" that contain the information of the whole universe. This kind of replication is very similar to the process and result by which a fertilized egg grows into an adult.

The homologous replication in the universe means that everything in the universe is a replica of the primitive atom before the big bang, and material information of the whole universe exists in any one universal hereditary gene. All phenomena in the universe are simply results of recessive and apparent changes of different combinations of the hereditary genes at a certain level. Therefore, in the universe, the information of the whole universe exists in living bodies and nonliving things everywhere and at any time. The universe is an inseparable totality in which each part is closely linked with the other. Any one part contains the information of the totality.

Harmony is the central law in the holographic universe. It protractedly and universally influences and determines the fate of everything in the universe. It is the same for nature, for living beings, and also for nonliving things. The power of Harmony directs all of nature, all living beings, and nonliving things. Therefore, the universe and nature as seen by us demonstrate exceptional harmony and order, in which everything survives and thrives.

Material Basis of the Culture of Harmony

We sow in spring and harvest in autumn. The cycle of a plant's life begins with the sowing of seeds and ends with the harvesting of fruits. This is the plant's holographic homologous replication. The births and deaths of human beings are holographic homologous replications of the lives of human beings. Let's also observe the brain of a human body. It commands all the body's internal organs. The arteries and veins of the four limbs crisscross in perfect order. When we observe ourselves, we cannot help but feel that such a system in the human body is just like a society. In reality, we may find such a truth; all socialized things—such as the information industry, the communication and transportation industry, and the workings of the Internet and other such systems—are a kind of apparent adaptation to the hidden social system in the human body and are also the socialization of the needs of the individuals involved in them. If the hidden societies in the human bodies did not have these needs, it would be impossible to create those socialized things. By this sense, social systems are inevitable results of the small societies of the holographic, homologous replicated human bodies. This is the materials basis of the Culture of Harmony.

Spiritual Basis of the Culture of Harmony

The spiritual basis of the Culture of Harmony is the practices of spiritual, homologous replication and awakening, in which human beings—in the process of long-term evolution—rapidly replicate various kinds of potential information capacities that they have already acquired and awaken them in a holographic form. This happens because, in daily life, it is not possible for us to personally experience everything we need to know to successfully navigate the world we are born into. Then how do infants understand those things that cannot be expressed by actions? As a lot of things cannot be explained in words, how do infants sense things and acquire sensing abilities? Scientists believe that human beings inherit sensing, holographic, homologous structures that are present in the brain from birth. Scientists have conducted experiments to prove this fact. They put some human babies and some chimpanzee infants together, cultivating and educating them. But whatever the researchers did, the chimpanzee infants could never learn human being's characteristic language and sense. The human babies, on the other hand, could very easily learn these in the process of their growth. The chimpanzees could only understand a few fixed or routine hints. This research demonstrates that the sensing structure of the human beings is formed in the process of the long-term spiritual, homologous replication and awakening. It is developed on the basis of information, the holographic resonance of which exists everywhere in the material world. They have internalized the resonance of this holographic information through spiritual, homologous replication and awakening. Since its beginnings, life has awakened, through experience, homologous information about adapting to various natural environments. It has gradually internalized this information as hereditary genes, forming holographic structures that are adaptable to specific natural environments. We know that the sensing, holographic structures of all human beings are identical. The sensing, homologous replication structure of every individual is the result of human awakening. Therefore, it is a holographic element of the awakening of human intelligence.

Horizontally speaking, the hologram of the cultural spirit of the Harmony of the universe and of human beings does not abstractly stay above human beings. Rather, it specifically exists within humanity's cultural spirit. In fact, the spirit of Harmony is a general trend formed by the human ability to coordinate and functions as cultural beings. So in fact, the Harmony of the universe is already hidden in the human cultural spirit and shows itself in the human ability to coordinate and live cohesively. The Harmony of the universe, in turn, leaves its own spiritual, homologous replication in human beings, thus rendering the human cultural spirit an epitome of the Harmony of the universe. So it is called the Culture of Harmony. The human Culture of Harmony shares the central law of universal Harmony in the form of spiritual, homologous replication and awakening. But the hologram of the Harmony within each individual person and the universal core law is different. So they are *harmonious and different.*

The Culture of Harmony in Human Civilization

Matter changes into spirit, and spirit changes into matter. Today, this has become common knowledge. But when we examine this exchange from the perspective of holographic, homologous replication and awakening, we also find that matter and spirit possess new and more profound meanings. Matter and spirit are different, but they are mutually connected and interchangeable. When people command the material world through spirit-to-matter and matter-to-spirit replication and awakening, matter will change into spirit. This is commonly known as spirit being a reflection of matter. However, spirit does not passively reflect the material world but, rather, it actively and dynamically does so. Under certain conditions, spirit can passively play a great role in the development of the material world.

Skyscrapers are repetitions of the holographic, homologous replication and awakening assumed by architects. Ten thousand-ton ships sail in the sea according to the will of the people. Space shuttles serve as "bridges" between Earth and space. Computers control "living" robots. All these man-made products and playgrounds of the man-made world are results of the homologous replication

5

between matter and spirit and the awakening of spirit; they are the materialization of spirit.

Now we may express the holographic, homologous matter-to-spirit replication and awakening in the following way: the homologous replication and awakening of matter and spirit are mutual. The man-made world is the result of the externalization of human spirit and of the holographic, homologous matter-to-spirit replication of the material world and awakening of human spirit. In fact, both the holographic common structures of the subjective world and of the artificial objective world exist because of matter's holographic, homologous replication and awakening toward spirit.

Harmony projects into the human civilization process in the form of holographic universal core law, which the ancient Chinese profoundly recognized long ago. Their ideological outlook—"The heaven and the earth are the big universe, and the human bodies are the small universe"—is a miniature of the theory by which the universal holographic, homologous replication awakens people and, thus, renders the human cultural spirit the Harmony of the universe. Furthermore, the structural chart of an atom in a grain of sand is very similar to the structural chart of the galaxy. This is a result of the universe being holographic; thus, we may reckon the unknown based on the known. Social systems are simply the externalized forms of the systems of the human bodies. Through the universal holographic, homologous replication and awakening, human beings have discovered the ordinary laws of development, the way that the spiritual world unifies with the material world, and the interactive forces between them.

Therefore, human beings (as well as everything else that exists in the world) are independent individuals, equally existing in the space of the universe, respecting the law that says we should be in harmony with the heaven, with the earth, with human beings, and with nature and that we should share and coexist prosperously. The Culture of

Harmony contains the idea of Harmony, the ethics of Harmony, the systems of Harmony, and the wisdom of Harmony, convering the natural, material facets and the humanistic, spiritual facets.

The concept of Harmony emerged very early in human history. It rooted in the farming civilization in the early period of the human beings, closely related to the people's material life in the early period. The Chinese character for harmony, 和, is composed of two parts—禾 (standing grain, especially rice) and 口 (mouth). An ancient Chinese book《说文》(*An Analytical Dictionary of Characters*) says, "人所言食也" ("What the people talk about is food"), indicating that the original meaning of 和 (harmony) was that grain satisfied human material needs of food, thus representing harmony of diet. Furthermore, in the *Chinese Calligraphy Dictionary*, the character 和 (harmony) originated from an ancient musical wind instrument, which produced very melodious sound. So the Chinese character 和 (harmony) in the earliest period represented "concord" and later derived into "tolerance" and "peace".

In Chinese history, we find many people who have made outstanding contributions to the process of the formation of Harmony as a kind of human spirit. From Rao's "harmonious nations," and Shi Bo's notions of "harmony" and "similarity" to Confucius's, "Harmony is invaluable," these contributions are widespread. The great Confucianist from Northern Song dynasty, Zhang Zai, professed, "Hatred must be solved by Harmony." Sun Yet-sen talked of "Great unity and Harmony." And Feng Youlan spoke of "Great Harmony."

Since the beginning of history, human beings have distinctively and deeply embraced the concept of Harmony and the spirit of Harmony, advocating Harmony, pursuing concord, and upholding peace. For years, human beings have related to and drawn strength from words that promote harmony—"peaceful coexistence," "work together with one accord in time of difficulties," "peaceful competition," "harmonious symbiosis," "harmonious coordination," "concord," "peaceful living," "harmony of people," "universal peace and harmony," and "compatibility," for example. The ancient Chinese culture deeply understood the meaning of Harmony. The ancient Chinese regarded it as the fundamental law of the universe. To them, Harmony was a thoroughfare under the heaven. When central Harmony was realized, heaven and earth would be in proper alignment and all things would grow well. Harmony is the fundamental guarantee of continuous prosperity of the universe. Every living being relies on Harmony. Harmony is the most important moral principle, especially the harmonious unity of two sides of a contradiction. Harmony has important political meaning. As the old saying goes, "Good timing is not as important as geographical convenience, and geographical convenience is not as important as harmonious human relations."

Rao was at his official position for seventy years, making outstanding administrative achievements. His greatest political goal was to realize a harmonious, prosperous society that harmonized all nations. In order to realize the latter part of this goal, he struggled arduously, exhausting his every capacity. Rao's idea of "harmonizing all nations" has deep roots in people's minds. Later, Confucius acknowledged and developed Shi Bo's viewpoint and stated, "Men of noble characters are harmonious with differences while mean persons are similar but are not harmonious." You Zi, one of Confucius's students, stated, "The benevolent love people. They regard Harmony as the most valuable way of dealing with others." Confucius and his Confucian school implemented the spirit of that ideal and designed a comfortably ideal society with universal harmony in the book entitled *The Book of Rites and the Application of Rites*. *The Great Learning*, one of "the Four Books" in Confucianism, talks about "cultivating one's moral character, keeping the family well, administering the country in good order and bringing peace to the world." This was the most explicit and most systematic programmatic doctrine of the Confucian school before the Qin Dynasty on constructing a harmonious society and a harmonious world. Chinese Confucian philosophers Mencius and Xun Zi both attached great importance to the role of Harmony among people.

Doctrine of the Mean, another of the Four Books, closely combines the concept of Harmony and the concept of center, forming a new concept of "Central Harmony" and states the ways and importance of realizing Central Harmony. "The state before the occurrence of happiness, anger, sorrow and enjoyment is called as 'centre'. The state after the occurrence of happiness, anger, sorrow and enjoyment is called as 'central joint' or Harmony. Centre is the great base of everything under the heaven. Harmony is a thoroughfare under the heaven. When the Central Harmony has been realized, the heaven and the earth are at good positions and all things grow well." Confucius and his Confucian school have made outstanding contributions toward ensuring that Harmony is the spiritual and systematic foundation of the Chinese nation. The Confucian school has passed on the torch of learning from teachers to students, never lacking successors in all the generations since its establishment.

Neo-Confucian moral philosopher, Zhang Zai, said, "When someone is doing something, there would be some opponents. As a result, hatred would exist. Hatred can be solved only by Harmony." Philosopher Feng Youlan fully affirmed and highly appraised these four dicta of Zhang Zai. He said, "Zhang Zai said: 'Hatred can be solved only by Harmony.' This word 'Harmony' is not casually used here." Harmony is an important domain in Zhang Zai's philosophical system. Zhang Zai held that both a society's normal state and that of the universe was Harmony. He called this Harmony "Great Harmony." He also had other four dicta—to be very much concerned about heaven and earth, to protect the lives of the average people, to succeed the profound learning of the sages of the past and of people of virtue, and to promote peace for the coming generations.

Dr. Sun Yat-sen, a great forerunner in the democratic revolution in modern times, created the theory of the Three Principles of People, emphasizing the nation, civil rights, and the livelihood of the people, in order to lead the bourgeois New Democratic Revolution. In Sun Yat-sen's philosophy, nationalism meant to fight against imperialism and uphold equality among all the ethnic groups at home. The principle of democracy forwarded the need to establish democratic policies that served ordinary citizens, not private interests of a small number of people. The principle of the people's livelihood spoke to the need to equalize the rights to possess land and to command and manage capital. Sun Yat-sen's theory of the Three Principles of People regarded a "perfect" society and a harmonious society as the highest aspiration in the field of social construction. He said, "What is the purpose of human evolution? That is just what Confucius said 'All the people walking on the roads are to work for the public benefits of the people under the heaven', 'a perfect world means that everyone works for the public benefits of the people under the heaven.'" Sun Yat-sen proposed that the principle of mutual assistance be the law for constructing a harmonious society. He said, "Species live on the principle of competition while the human beings live on the principle of mutual assistance. The society and the nation are organizations for realizing mutual assistance. The morality and virtue are for being applied in the mutual assistance. To stick to this principle, human beings would be prosperous, otherwise they would perish. This principle should have been applied by the human beings for several hundred thousand years." Although Sun Yat-sen's revolution did not succeed, he unyieldingly made the construction of a harmonious society his goal, a goal he struggled relentless to achieve throughout his lifetime.

The Culture of Harmony, cultivated by human beings in the long-term process of social development in various historical periods, is now continuously developing.

CHAPTER TWO

———

THE CONCEPT AND DOMAIN OF HARMONY

Harmony as a World Outlook

Over the course of human development, two major ideological systems have formed as to whether matter or consciousness existed first. The materialist ideological system held that matter was primary in the world, while the idealist ideological system claimed that consciousness came first. Which of the two major ideological systems was right or wrong? Endless debates that have been ongoing for several thousand years have never reached consensus. Human cognition continuously deepens, and the degree of human civilization continuously increases, especially with the emergence of high-tech capabilities. The concept of Harmony has emerged as the times require. In the Chinese language, the character 宇 (yǔ) means "the upper side, the down side, the east side, the south side, the west side, and the north side," while the Chinese character 宙 (zhòu) means "through the ages." When we put 宇 and 宙 together, we have 宇宙. These two characters mean "universe." The universe is a unity of time and space, matter and consciousness. Harmony, as the core law of the universe, exists above matter and consciousness. It is a world outlook and a methodology that allows people to understand and transform the world. As a supreme ideological system, Harmony contains the following domains:

I. HARMONY

The so-called Harmony is a struggle and is also a unifier. It is a means and also a purpose. It is the unity of a spear and a buckler that together form contradiction. For example, we put a five-year-old child, a five-year-old chimpanzee, and a five-year-old monkey in the same school. Later, the child successfully learns something, while neither the chimpanzee nor the monkey learns anything. This is because the ability to learn knowledge exists in the human body; it is a human instinct. We simply awaken this ability through education. The chimpanzee and the monkey don't have these kinds of genes to be awakened. Thus, by this logic, excessively emphasizing that matter is primary or consciousness is primary would become a phenomenon much like a husband who claims he is reasonable while his wife says she is reasonable, never having any results. Only the theory of Harmony tells us that all things in the world are harmonious and different.

II. COMMONALITIES

What are commonalities? They are fields wherein things link with each other, supplement each other, and interact on each other. This field phenomenon exists in all things in the world, and it exists in the entirety of any development process. Commonalities exist anytime and anywhere. For example, in the process of human development in the past several thousand years, common genes have always existed. Those who possess human attributes are all called human beings. "Human attributes" are simply the commonalities of human beings.

We can extend this theory to the rest of existence. For example, plants, no matter how diverse or seemingly different they are, so long as they possess the attributes of plants, are called plants. Their shared attributes are simply the commonalities of plants. In the vast world, no matter how varied or complicated things are, we can find the commonalities among them.

III. Differences

What are differences? Differences are the particularities that vary from a base of common attributes. The vast world is composed simply by these kinds of particularities. For example, researchers divide people living in the current world—who all possess common attributes—into more than 2,500 ethnic groups. These ethnic groups have different languages, different customs, and different cultural ins and outs. The differences are the reason why so many ethnic groups exist in the world.

In sum, the world is gradually developing through *seeking major commonalities while maintaining minor differences and seeking minor commonalities while maintaining major differences*, on the basis of Harmony. We will return to this concept.

Harmony as a Methodology

Harmony is a great guide to the development of human civilization in the contemporary ear. Harmony between nature and human beings creates ecological balance. Harmony in the family brings about prosperity. Harmony between collectives and individuals maintains social stability. Harmony among ethnic groups promotes national rejuvenation. Harmony among religions and nations builds world peace.

HARMONY BETWEEN NATURE AND HUMAN BEINGS CREATES ECOLOGICAL BALANCE

Human beings and nature are related to each other, supplement each other, and affect each other. Only when human beings respect nature will nature respect human beings. If human beings do not properly handle their relationship with nature, they will damage the Harmony between human beings and nature. For example, environmental problems such as global warming and carbon emissions are forcing us to seriously study the Harmony between human beings and nature. Human beings must understand nature in order to realize Harmony between nature and human beings and to resolve the ecological crises we are facing. People should be friendly with nature, attach importance to nature, express their feelings to nature, and comprehend nature.

Social Harmony consists of three layers of progressive relationships—relationships between human beings and nature, among individual human beings, and between human beings and society. When we talk about Harmony, we should first talk about Harmony between the human beings and nature. This is the most fundamental Harmony. We may say that without this Harmony, there would be no way of talking about any other Harmonies. Since the time when anthropoid apes evolved into human beings who could make tools, the relationship between the human society and nature began to entail complex overlapping. Although human beings create for themselves a world that is totally different from that of nature, the world of their creation, "the world-for-themselves," still relies on nature, "the world-in-itself." Therefore, human beings are products of the world-in-itself and are also creators of the world-for-themselves. What kind of relationship should human beings establish between themselves and nature? This question relates to the fate of human beings and the fate of the earth on which human beings have been living. People's continuous exploration and self-examination in regards to the relationship between themselves and nature are the theoretical prerequisites that we are to study and that we must think deeply about.

Two Consequences of Utilizing Natural Resources

The entire history of humankind is, in a sense, a history of utilizing natural resources. As human beings increase the ability to utilize natural resources, so does their level of productivity. However, the course of humanity's utilization of natural resources has not always been smooth.

To respect nature and to do things following the rules of nature will benefit humankind. Let's talk about the atmospheric layer. Currently, human beings are still not able to control the atmospheric environment. The energy released by one typhoon is equivalent to that released by two hundred 20,000-ton atomic bombs. Human beings cannot weaken a typhoon, but people can predict its path, thus reducing its damage. With the advancement of productivity and deeper understanding of natural laws, the scales of human utilization of nature have been continuously expanding and continuously turning to the direction of utilizing nature conscientiously. Over the long period of human production, people have transformed and utilized nature in countless ways and have accumulated rich experiences, culminating in the ability to utilize nature to benefit humankind to certain extents. On the contrary, nature will inevitably punish those who go against its laws. While they have utilized natural laws to benefits society, people have also done many things that violated natural laws. During the period when science and technology were not well developed, people's knowledge was limited; they pursued short-term benefits of utilizing nature and failed to see the long-term effects abusing nature. With scientific and technological development, the pursuit of short-term economic efficiency in the fields of superstructure and management systems has created outstanding contradictions between human beings and nature, resulting in punishment from nature. For example, improper reclamation of land and denudation of forest have caused and will inevitably continue to cause deterioration of water and land resources. In many regions in the world today, damage of water and land resources has become one of the main hurdles affecting the regions' ability to produce and develop.

Evolution of the Relationship between Human Beings and Nature

The history of the development of human society is also the history of human beings and nature, which moved from primitive Harmony to separation, opposition, and confrontation to Harmony and coordinated development. Human beings and nature are a contradiction. The relationship between human beings and nature is an everlasting topic from time immemorial and will continue to be to the future. It reflects the interaction of human civilization and the natural evolution and reveals the dialectical development process in which the existence and development of human society rely on nature, change nature, and influence the structure and functions of nature.

A. In the stage of the primitive society, the relationship between human beings and nature showed a character of general Harmony. In the coexistence of human beings and nature, the main side or the guiding functional side of the contradiction was nature. Changes in the natural environment forced some apes to come down from the trees and live on the ground. After evolving into human beings who could make tools, humankind separated itself from the animal kingdom and developed independently, forming two major features—the ability to walk upright and increased brain capacities. Their physique changed greatly. These are so-called human biotic adaptation. The making of tools and the use of fire are so-called human cultural adaptation. In their development, these two adaptations changed as the natural environment changed. Based on all this, human beings evolved and human society appeared. But due to mankind's low level of productivity, the products of the natural environment in the primitive society, such as fish in the water, birds in the sky, wild vegetables and wild fruits in the forests and fields, were necessary conditions to maintain the existence of the primitive human beings. At that time humankind could only passively live in the natural environment. So in the primitive society, the harmony of the relationship between human beings and nature was manifested as humankind's reverence and passive obedience toward nature. The guiding factor of the harmony between human beings and nature could only be nature. Nature determined the survival and advancement of humankind.

B. In the stage of the farming society, the relationship between the human beings and nature was still generally harmonious. It is noteworthy that this kind of general harmony was already beginning to change. That is to say, from a foundation of general harmony, discontinuous and regional disharmony had emerged. Due to the increase of human population and the gradual advancement of productivity, humankind grew discontented with the protection and rule of nature. While utilizing nature, people attempted to transform and change nature. Due to the lack of understanding of nature and the slow development of science and technology, such transformation and changes were, to a great extent, indiscriminate, random, and destructive. In the farming era, because the population increase was slow, the total population wasn't great, and natural resources were relatively abundant. Thus, human destruction of nature was only discontinuous and regional. Meanwhile, humanity also started to develop the idea of conforming to nature.

C. In the stage of industrial civilization, the relationship between human beings and nature was, in general, out of balance. Since the advent of industrial civilization until the 1960s, the human conception of nature changed with advancement in science and technology and development of social productivity. The dominant view changed from "utilizing nature" to "conquering nature." Hence, human beings viewed themselves as the masters of nature, capable of making laws for nature. Some scholars claimed that, with the help of science, we could make ourselves masters and governors of nature. Very great changes took place in the relationship between human beings and nature. Humankind's desire to conquer and rule nature resulted in the plundering and destruction of nature. People relentlessly consumed natural resources, resulting in the discharge of a huge amount of pollutants. The catastrophic consequences, such as the depletion of certain natural resources, the continuous deterioration of ecology, the energy crisis, the environmental pollution, the shortage of water, the global warming, the desertification of land, and the large-scale extinction of plant and animal species, seriously threatened human survival and advancement.

D. In the postindustrial stage of civilization, humanity's understanding of its relationship with nature has generated a new leap forward. Hopefully, humanity will realize harmony in its relationship with nature under the guidance of the concepts of human orientation and scientific development. While human beings gained immense fortune by conquering nature, they also created tremendous disasters. This has forced humankind to reflect on its relationship with nature. Now the global governance has become a common view of various nations. On June 5, 1972, the United Nations released the first programmatic document in the world on maintaining and improving the environment. The Declaration on Human Environment and Development stated seriously that humankind has only one earth. While developing and utilizing nature, humankind also has the responsibility of protecting nature. Humankind and the environment comprise a union that cannot be severed. In February 1987, the World Commission of Environment and Development presented to the United Nations a report entitled *Our Common Future, From One Earth to One World: Report of the World Commission on Environment and Development.* The report put forward the concept of "sustainable development" and made what, up until now, has been the most authoritative definition of "sustainable development." Sustainable development is development that meets the needs of the current generation and will not constitute harm to the abilities of the coming generations to meet their needs. Since then the theory of sustainable development has lived deeply in people's hearts. Hence, human society also started a new course of development. Since then, a series of programmatic documents and international conventions with milestone significance were successively promulgated, marking that realizing harmonious development of human beings and nature has become a global consensus. Under the

21

condition of conducting global, comprehensive governance, we can anticipate the harmonious development of human beings and nature.

The Cognitive Root of the Disharmony between Human Beings and Nature

Harmonious development is the ideal state of the relationship between human beings and nature, but the harmonious development of this relationship is not static. Social progress and scientific and technological development have been changing the relationship between human beings and nature incessantly. This relationship continuously advances along the curving course of "harmony–disharmony–new harmony." Recalling the complex course of humanity's historical understanding of its relationship with nature, we can see that the imbalance of the relationship has profound cognitive roots.

A. *The Influence of Human Centralism.* The development of the industrial society brought about rapid increases to the level of human productivity. While creating enormous material fortune for humankind, this development also led to an inflation of human ego, causing extremely narrow philosophies of human centralism. Human centralism held that humankind was the center of all things; human beings were both the subjects of value and those who could make value judgments. This understanding held that all things should regard the interests and values of human beings as starting points, ignoring the fact that human existence must have nature's sustainable existence as a premise. As a result, humankind audaciously, recklessly, and madly exercised plunder and destruction of nature, damaging the harmony between humanity and nature and jeopardizing the fundamental interests of humankind. Today, some developed countries continue to export industries that contaminate the environment and destroy nature irreversibly to economically backward countries and regions for the sake of their own interests, disregarding the interests of the whole of humankind. In many places in the world, the phenomenon that some people recklessly destroy the environment in order to gain short-term economic interests exists. This extreme human centralism has led to global ecological imbalance and environmental pollution and, hence, is finally threatening the existence and development of the human society. For example, the threat of bird flu and some other epidemic diseases to humankind is a result of the imbalance of the relationship between human beings and nature and is leading to nature's revenge against mankind.

B. *The Complexity of the Relationship between Human Beings and Nature Leads to the Deviation of Human Understanding.* The complexity of the relationship between human beings and nature leads to the deviation of human understanding. On the one hand, human understanding of nature, due to the limitation of subjective and objective conditions, will inevitably go through a complex process. This is the subjective cause leading to humanity's failure to correctly understand nature. Because the essence of nature is an incessantly moving and changing process, human understanding of the circulating law of the ecosystem is also developing with twists and turns. During the primitive society and the farming era, two fundamental causes led to nature controlling and enslaving human beings—humankind's limited productivity and lack of knowledge, which led to human ignorance of and reverence to nature. Since the Industrial Revolution, with its scientific and technological advances, humanity has improved its capacity to adapt to and understand nature. However, human beings went to the other extreme, exaggerating human influence over nature and regarding humanity as nature's master, transforming and conquering nature at will. Humankind used advanced science and technology to excessively exploit, utilize, and transform nature, causing tremendous damage to nature. Nature's self-cleaning capacity is deteriorated day after day, making nature increasingly inappropriate for human beings to live in. On the other hand, in the course of solving concrete problems and contradictions, the activities of humans would involve many kinds of complex relationships. Although in the world, the international community has already reached an initial consensus on the importance of correctly handling the relationship between human beings and nature, the conflicts of interest in fields such as ideology, politics, diplomacy, military affairs, economy, and culture among various nations are still rather complicated. We still have a long way to go before implementing the consensus into concrete actions. There exist a lot of differences in the conditions of various areas. The contradictions and conflicts between efficiency and fairness, between becoming rich first and becoming rich later, between the interests of one part of the community and the interests of the whole community, and between the long-term interests and the short-term interests, are extremely obvious. Humankind once experienced a roundabout course where people pursued economic efficiency one-sidedly, sacrificing the environment in the pursuits of ridding society of poverty, fast development and harnessing the environment after achieving economic development. Not a few regions have even brought about serious consequences that can never be remedied for short-term and present benefits. Although we now already have relatively clear understanding, it is not easy to completely eradicate those wrongdoings. We must make great efforts.

A Change of Mind-set Is the Premise for Realizing a Harmonious Relationship between Human Beings and Nature

Reality has told us that, in order to realize our target production capability, rich life, and good ecology, we must correctly handle the relationship between human beings and nature. We must change some old, outdated, and one-sided concepts; establish the correct concepts of humankind's relationship with earth, of our value system, and of the ethics of our production goals; and realize a harmonious relationship between human beings and nature.

A. *We Must Change the Belief That Human Beings Are the Masters of Nature.* This concept of the relationship between humankind and earth is based on the idea that human society is antagonistic to nature; that the development of human society is the process of conquering and plundering nature; and that the more we get from nature, the greater material fortune we will have and the higher degree of material civilization we will achieve. This concept has led to the human plunder of nature and the daily deterioration of the ecological environment. Humanity must understand that nature is the cornerstone that supports the mansion of human civilization and the foundation on which human society emerged and developed. To plunder nature is to plunder the future of human society. Human society is a product of the long-term development of nature. To realize the harmonious coexistence of human beings and nature, we must fully understand that natural resources are limited; we should wrest natural resources only in cycles that are healthy for the environment. We must not allow the wastes generated as a result of our industries and daily life to become greater than nature's ability to clean itself.

Cherishing resources and protecting the environment are the indispensable responsibilities of humankind.

B. *We Must Change the Concept of Placing High Value on Consumerism and Hedonism.* As social production makes continuous progress, people's pursuit of materials increases progressively. People want more high-end products, and their needs go from simple stability to complex changeability. These kinds of changes in consumption, on the one hand, reflect humanity's economic and social progress. On the other hand, consumerism and hedonism gradually dominate people's economic and social lives. As productive forces rapidly increase, material wealth increases sharply. In certain periods, people have formed the fictitious belief that supply exceeds demand. Thus, consumerism and hedonism also spread everywhere. When society values these concepts, people's spiritual satisfaction is totally based on material consumption and their dignity becomes equal with their ability to consume. This is especially true of the massive, overindulgent consumption that forms the mentality of nouveau riche, in which wealthy people are those who wantonly squander resources, and the wanton squandering of material wealth is the expression of being rich. This kind of mentality dispels and even twists the true meaning of the spirit of all cultural activities in human society. To establish correct values, we must express our own happiness in moderate consumption, seeking a balancing between consumption and sensible demand and using our rational faculty to understand that human beings should restrict the desire to consume in a way that expands without limits. We must also require people to base their consumption on a level that conforms to a balance between a healthy level of material production and ecological well-being. We must meet people's consumption needs on the premise of protecting the ecological environment and ensuring that people's consumption is appropriate, sustainable, well-rounded, and coordinated, with spiritual consumption as primary motivator.

C. *We Must Change the Old Production Mindset.* In the eras of primitive civilization, farming civilization, and industrialization, production was regarded as a means for obtaining basic living materials—as activities engaged in so as to meet one's individual needs. In a sense, these are important causes of the damage suffered by the natural ecosystems. Placing the protection of nature and the environment in the domain of production and developmental industries, forwarding the concept of green GDP, and establishing circular economy are good steps toward ensuring that humanity only utilizes nature under the premise of understanding, respecting, and protecting nature and loving all things under the sun. Such steps will ensure that humankind and all things in nature mutually exchange materials and energy under highly harmonious unity, so that we can finally realize harmonious development of humanity alongside the natural ecosystem.

D. *We Must Change the Outdated "Good" and "Evil" Concept of Ethics.* Any social structure has an ethical system that supports its members and is compatible to their needs. Different social structures have different understandings of the concepts of good and evil, and each must realize harmonious ethics that its members generally approve. In the vision of harmonious ethics in modern society, we can no longer obtain our greatest happiness through arbitrarily controlling all things in nature, but rather, we must use our harmonious rational faculty to promote the balanced development of all things. Human beings can be benevolent only when they have become sources favorable to harmony between people and nature; otherwise they are evil. The daily deterioration of the ecological system actually reflects the human ethical crisis. The natural ecosystem is an integrated unity formed over billions of years. In this system, all life has both a certain position and the right to sustainable survival. A harmonious and orderly ecosystem is the prerequisite for the existence and development of human society. Only when all things in nature are included in human's understanding of social, ethical Harmony can the relationship between human beings and nature realize true harmonious development. Humankind cannot survive without the earth. The conflicts between human beings and nature are reflected in the lack of protection of the environment and ecology. A fine and appropriate environment and ecology will provide a powerful guarantee for the sustainable development of human society. After entering the twenty-first century, people are increasingly supportive of the notion that we must protect the environment and the earth's resources. Comprehensive control of the methodology for using those resources, the restoration of farmland to forest, the retrieval of grasslands from grazing, and the protection of ecological balance are all important measures toward correcting the mistakes in the relationship between human beings and nature. The central goal is to try to achieve a sustainable benign cycle of environment, ecosystem, society, and economy and, ultimately, realizing harmony between nature and humanity.

HARMONY IN THE FAMILY BRINGS ABOUT PROSPERITY

Families are basic units of the social structure and the primary force that maintains national stability. Whether families are harmonious or not is of critical importance to social harmony. This is because families are the cells that form a nation; a nation is comprised of thousands and thousands of families. If some families are not harmonious, they are not united. This may lead to many families being inharmonious. If this was the case, talk of social and national harmony would be empty. The members in a family, including the parents, the sons and daughters, the brothers and sisters, the husband and the wife, should unite and love each other. This is a prerequisite to social harmony. Wise men of past generations attached great importance to harmony of families. Why? There are three reasons.

Firstly, a nation is closely linked with families, just like a body is closely linked to the blood and flesh within it. Judging from the origins of human societies, families originated earlier than nations. As early as in the matriarchal society of ancient times when there were no kings and kingdoms, families with mothers as centers emerged. In primitive societies, human beings "dwelled in woods and rock caves" and "wandered among swine and deer" without any of the fixed organizations we have today. Later, families gradually emerged. People had families. That made it possible for them to have dwellings. Due to the multiplication of family population, the areas where people lived expanded and, hence, big clans were formed. Later a number of clans formed a nation. We often talk about nations and families. Judging from the fact that we mention nation first and then families, we can ascertain that we place higher importance on the former. If we think of the origin of these structures, we should mention families first. As the saying goes, "A nation is an enlarged family, while a family is a reduced nation."

Secondly, as a nation is formed by thousands and thousands of families, the interests of the nation should conform to the interests of most families. The nation should safeguard the interests of its families, while it's a universally accepted principle that each family should safeguard the interests of the nation. For example, when facing an enormous natural disaster, a single family cannot possibly resist the disaster on its own. The nation should organize resources to provide relief to families who suffered from the disaster. In the same vein, when a nation is invaded, families are duty bound to help fight against foreign invasion. Doing this safeguards the families and defends the nation. It is also a way of loving the nation and its citizens—of safeguarding the national administration and national interests, as well as safeguarding the interests of the individuals and the families that comprise the nation.

Thirdly, emphasis on Harmony in families generally cultivates people's moral qualities. If there are great emotional attachments among family members, people care for and love each other. This is conducive to cultivating important qualities, such as caring for, loving, and tolerating other members of society and being honest and modest, as well as to restricting inflation of selfish desires. The forming of these fine qualities does not rely on external pressure. It's not necessary to run any special training classes. Rather, we can rely on people's self-discipline and their ability to gradually form these mental habits during their long-term practice of being a member of a family member day and night. A person is both a family member and a member of society. In a society, regardless of whether a person is an official or an ordinary citizen, he or she needs to have these important moral qualities when contacting other people. Just as Richard Taylor of UNESCO said in his message to the Academic Conference on Commemorating the 2,540th Anniversary of the Birthday of Confucius, "Confucius praised highly families and the mutual love and mutual respect needed to establish fine and perfect families. The family units are established on the bases of that kind of basic relations among parents, sons and daughters, and brothers and sisters. Similarly, the links of this kind of relations also exist between leaders of a nation and the nation's citizens. This kind of relationship is especially reflected in mutual love, mutual respect and restricting oneself. Our world urgently needs these."

How do we cultivate family harmony? Harmony cannot be realized by just one or two slogans. This kind of harmony is realized through cultural deposition of hundreds of generations for more than a thousand years, strictly requiring each family member to fulfill his or her own responsibilities and obligations; thusly, the fathers are righteous, the mothers are kind, the elder brothers and sisters are friendly, the younger brothers and sisters are respectful, and the children show filial obedience to their parents. The governance of a nation needs to put family harmony first, specifying the obligations that the fathers, mothers, elder siblings, and children should fulfill. Thus can we realize a society in which fathers and sons are dear to each other, monarchies and subjects are righteous to each other, husbands and wives play different roles, the youth respect their elders, and friends are faithful to each other. Parents are to love and protect their children, and children are to love and respect their parents. Monarchies must be just, while subjects must be faithful. Husbands must be righteous and shoulder the heavy burdens for the families, while wives must be obedient, acting as good helpers. Elder siblings must love and protect their younger siblings, while younger siblings must respect their elder siblings. Friends must be faithful in their contacts. Family members must love each other, respect each other, and unite in harmony, restricting their own selfish desires, fulfilling their own responsibilities, and making their own contributions.

In the matriarchal society of prehistoric times, people especially loved and respected their mothers, and hence the phenomenon of filial piety occurred. After entering a period when children knew both their mothers and fathers, they began to love and respect their fathers and mothers, and thus the concept of filial piety expanded. Love and respect that children have for their parents is called filial piety. Ancient people cultivated filial piety as a socially important virtue. When selecting officials and judging whether someone was good or evil, they first looked at the person's filial piety. The value of filial piety has been passed on from generation to generation. It unites members of a family, realizing harmony and unity among them. Thus are harmony and unity spread to the whole society, rendering thousands and thousands of families harmonious and united. We can deduce that one can rule a nation by filial piety. When filial piety is at society's core, families and the clans can be united vertically, while horizontally spreading to society and helping to achieve harmony in the entire nation. Social ethics are based on families, while family ethics are based on the individual's internal, natural filial piety and fraternal love. This is basic knowledge. The cultivation of all kinds of virtues cannot be separated from love and respect. The love between parents and their children is the most sincere attribute that human beings possess. The act of giving birth to and raising children is unselfish. Parents are happy to bear the hardships. Requiring children to show their filial piety and to repay their parents' generosity is also perfectly justified. Judging from the perspective of great righteousness, monarchies come before fathers and nations come before families. If we judge from the perspective of origin, we see that families come before nations. Filial piety is the origin of loyalty.

Today people's material living standards have improved unprecedentedly. However, in the mighty torrent of the temptation of money and material desires, traditional virtues have been broken down into great confusion: In order to satisfy personal material desires, some people don't attend to their parents, and others desert their wives and children. Some brothers become enemies. Some people kill their kinfolk and commit crimes. The disharmony in families causes serious social instability. The kind of people who do not even love their own parents and children will, by no means, love friends or other people. It is impossible for them to possess any good virtues. Many crimes actually originate in families. Harmony in families relies on good moral qualities of each member of the family. We must attach great importance to cultivating traditional virtues and to the harmony of traditional families. Harmony in families is the basis of social harmony. Harmonious families will bring about the success of many things.

Harmony between Collectives and Individuals Maintains Social Stability

The essence of human beings is the sum of social relations. When the interests of an individual and the interests of a collective are contradictory, the interests of the individual should subordinate to the interests of the collective, while the interests of the collective should make full allowance for the interests of the individual; thus harmony between the individual and the collective can form. Only harmony between individuals and the collectives can maintain social stability.

Human history tells the story of human activities. Furthermore, history tells the story of the activities of people who each have their own purposes. In other words, human beings are the most important factors, or the subjects of historic developments. The decisive factors of historic processes, in essense, are production and reproduction. Without human beings, no human production or reproduction is possible. Where there are human beings, there will be problems related to individuals and collectives. These are the core problems of political and ethical philosophy; in relation to the progress of the modern social civilization, these problems have important ethical dimensions. The Oriental traditional ethics have always attached importance to collectives while neglecting individuals when dealing with problems between collectives and individuals. Only in recent times have we seen discussions on issues related to boundaries between the rights of collectives and individuals. Western utilitarianism attaches importance to these boundaries, putting more emphasis on individualism when dealing with issues between the two. But its boundaries are difficult to operate. Harmony advocates a positive, virtuous interaction between collectives and individuals, guaranteeing the subjects freedom of creativity.

In a harmonious society, the collective ranges and the individual ranges should respect each other. The market economic system, on the one hand, broke the former interest structure. On the other hand, it has increased the number of both subjects and collectives with economic interests, forming a plural interest structure. The conflicts between the two have resulted in an unprecedentedly complex situation. Among these complex contradictions, the conflicts between collectives and individuals are especially prominent. Conducting in-depth discussions on issues between collectives and individuals from the political, ethical perspective is not only necessary to construct a healthy political arena and realize the pressing objective of the contemporary era—the establishment of a harmonious society—it is also necessary in order to avoid damages and losses that will result from the confusion surrounding collective and individual ranges and social development.

A. *The Important Ethical Dimensions of a Harmonious Society.*
We can look at the concept of harmony between collectives
and individuals and its relationship to a harmonious society
from different angles and arrive at different understandings of
this concept, but social development exists and is predicated
on the activities of human beings as social subjects. History
is simply the story of the activities of people pursuing their
purposes. Therefore, the state of social harmony, in essense,
is the state of harmony among social subjects (individuals
and collectives). The primary harmony is the one between
a collective and the individuals that comprise it. Social
subjects do not exist independently, but rather they exist
in the relations. The relationship between a collective and
individuals consists of three parts:

The first relationship is the one *between "the self as knower"*
and "the self as known." This means that an individual can
both evaluate him or herself and give him or herself orders. A
person is acting as "the self as knower" when he or she reacts
to other people's attitudes. Acting as "the self as known"
means adopting other people's attitudes. The dialectical unity
of "the self as knower" and "the self as known" means that
individuals do not inactively or passively conform to social
norms but, rather, take the initiative to make choices and to
achieve self-undertaking; thus individuals who participate in
social activities consciously generate a sense of responsibility
for their behavior. This process is also a process of moving
away from self-centeredness. When "the self as knower" and
"the self as known" fail to coordinate and unify—remaining
separate and isolated—"the looking glass self" will often
be blurred, thus lacking proper prioritizing of one's duties,
responsibilities, rights, and interests. A society in which the

35

subjects are not able to clearly know their own roles and identities will not possibly develop harmoniously.

Secondly, we find the relationship *between "me" and "him"*. Real subjects can possibly exist only when the subjects recognize and respect each other in the course of their contacts.

Thirdly, we find the relationship *between individuals and collectives*. In modern society, the development of individuals conforms to the development of society. In the ideal stage of development, free individuals live in a society based on a foundation wherein their all-around development and common social capacities have become their social wealth. To respect subjects and to create conditions that promote the all-around development of individuals are goals of social progress and social harmony. On issues related to collectives and individuals, the Oriental traditional ethic has always stressed collectives and neglected individuals, emphasizing the obligations and responsibilities of individuals to collectives, submerging the interests of individuals in the interests of collectives, and melting individuals into collectives. When studying Oriental traditional holism, we should not neglect the following two points:

- First, traditional Oriental ethical thought emphasizes "human sympathy," interweaving ethical outlook, universe outlook, and epistemology to form a model of "heaven and human integration." This model forms the Oriental spiritual foundation. When this foundation is expressed in the relationship between nature and human beings, between collectives and individuals, and between an individual and other people, the result is the harmonious unity of people and nature, people and society, and people and people. This also incorporates the integration of heaven and people, the unity of materials and individuals, and the harmony of individuals and other people.

- Second, the patriarchal clan system, in which the Oriental ancient social structure used blood lineage as links, existed for a long period of time. The concept that the whole country was one's family property, the clan system, and similar structures in families, linked with a patriarchal clan system that was maintained by "the rites," formed an autocratic and patriarchal clan system that was rigidly stratified. Individuals could give obedience only to public authorities, to national integrity, and to rulers of whom they were representatives. The existence and development of individuals must be turned around according to the need of the development of national integrity. The Confucius school's principle of integrity, through manipulation of the monarch dictatorship, changed into the theory of moral determination, emphasizing morality and justice, and the theory of ethic values, stressing spiritual realm. Relying on the relations of blood ties and lineages forms, maintains, and consolidates the collective-oriented holism. A nation was an enlarged ruling clan. The families and the nation were driven by the same sense of integrity. And hence, "the hearts, the ideology, the bodies, the families, the nation, the world under the heaven, the universe and the heaven above all the material things" were linked and formed an image of integrity, hatching the spirit of holism with cohesive forces. Chinese traditional holism played an active role in realizing feudal social control, coordinating relationships among people, and promoting the cohesion and development of the Chinese nation. But because it ignored individuals and made peace with despotism and the principle of the royal right, its role in the course of the nation's development became increasingly negative. In terms of social political control, it led to autocratic politics. In terms of social life, it led to conservative individual character, constraint, and restriction of creativity. In terms of social structural development, it led to individuals cutting themselves off from the outside world, thus rendering the changing of Chinese traditional society into a modern one a very difficult transition.

Since Democritus, an ancient Greece philosopher, established utilitarianism, utilitarian thought has been the main stream in the history of Western ethical thought. In our exploration, we can find reasonable tracks of the thought.

First, we find *the attaching of importance to individual interests*. French philosopher Claude Adrien Helvétius explicitly put forward the utilitarian ethical principles, holding that the core issue in human ethics was the issue of interests. He wrote, "In the world, interests are powerful wizards. They change the forms of all things before the eyes of all lives." There is no life without interests. It is even more the case that there exist no ethics which throw interests away and emerge independently. "If someone loves virtue but cannot get any interests, there would not be any virtue."

Secondly, we find *the understanding of the limits of selfishness, self-benefit, and self-love.* When English philosopher Thomas Hobbes claimed that the relationship between people was such that "man is man's wolf," "man's self-preservation" was human nature, and self-benefit and self-love were the basis of ethics, people in various places immediately criticized and opposed his concepts. Scottish philosopher and historian David Hume pointed out that human beings had sociality in addition to their selfish nature. He said, "Humankind are animals having the strongest desire for social combination in the universe, and have the most favorable conditions appropriate for social combination. Whenever we have a hope, we always cannot but look into the society. The state of complete isolation perhaps is the greatest punishment that we may come across."

Thirdly, we find *the view that individuals' personal interests are the basis for realizing social interests.* The logical starting point of the utilitarian principle of English philosopher Jeremy Bentham is, "It is pointless to talk about social interests without understanding individuals' interests." So when he emphasized, "When people approve or disapprove any behavior, the criteria are whether it increases or decreases the doer's level of happiness," "the principle of the greatest happiness of the largest majorities of the people" may be understood as the principle of "the greatest interests of the greatest number of individuals." Bentham's philosophy takes into account the survival tactics of social subjects, so it is, to a certain extent, practical and reasonable.

Fourthly, we find *the demarcation of collective and individual rights.* British philosopher John Stuart Mill inherited and further developed the philosophy of utilitarianism. In *On Liberty*, he put forward a utilitarian principle—the principle of demarcating collectives and individuals. First, so long as a personal behavior does not involve other people, there is no need to explain it to society. Neither other people nor society has the right to interfere. Second, if a personal behavior involves other people, the individual must explain his or her behavior to other people or society. If needed, both other people and society have the right to interfere. In other words, there must be clear limits or demarcations between personal interests and social interests and between personal rights and the power of the nation or a government. That is to say, regardless of whether we're talking about a person, society, the nation or a government, one's behavior should not violate or harm other's interests and rights.

Obviously, the traditional Oriental holism theory on morality and justice neglects the individuals' existence, while the Western utilitarianism theory on collectives and individuals attaches importance to individuals and attempts to establish demarcations for collective and individual rights. But this kind of demarcations of rights mainly focuses on the part of individuals, publicizing the individuals' positions, while neglecting to acknowledge the fact that people in a society are always in relationships and have contacts between whom there are mutual influences and, thus, the demarcations of collective and individual rights are fuzzy and partial. On the other hand, its definition of individual freedom and its discussions on solutions for the violation of freedom are incomplete. So the utilitarian demarcation of collective and individual rights lacks feasibility in practice. To sum up, realistic approaches to raising the collective and individual sense of harmony include using the theory of morality and justice to supplement and perfect the defects of utilitarianism and using the strong points of utilitarianism to amend the shortcomings of the theory of morality and justice—in other words, combining virtue, joy, and happiness.

B. *Realizing Harmony between Collectives and Individuals: From a Just Society to a Harmonious Society.* Judging from the angle of collective-individual relationship, the social development experiences two stages: the just society stage and the harmonious stage. In terms of rights that the individuals have, the just society guarantees both the subjects' passive freedom and the subjects' active freedom, while the harmonious society guarantees the subjects' freedom of creativity.

A so-called just society, on the one hand, it first of all needs to guarantee the individuals' freedom, their lives and properties not being harmed by the state or any collectives. Because this kind of freedom is the individuals' basic freedom, is the basic guarantee for maintaining the individuals' survival and practice activities, and is also the basic condition to maintain human beings as human beings. This can be called as the individuals' "passive freedom". In a society or under a political regime, if certain social organs or public organizations impose restrictions on private-domain freedom of citizens, or even conduct insulting harms on citizens' rights or interests such as humanity dignity. Under autocratic regimes, there is almost no guarantee for citizens' dignity and for preventing them being insultingly harmed. For example, in the Chinese dynasties of feudal centralism, "If a monarch wants a subject to die, the subject has to die."

Various kinds of brutal tortures and cruel laws glared like tigers eyeing the citizens as their prey, no individuals' rights being safeguarded. However, human beings, just because that they are human beings, only when they enjoy status of human beings can they win respects. In a society where the legal system is not perfect, private domains often suffer from restriction or violation by public power, while collective (public) domains, including "the public power" itself, are often controlled by individual will and small groups' interests. A society where there is no freedom in private domains and there is no democracy in public domains would not be able to guarantee the spirit and mind of the citizens being prevented from being insulted.

On the other hand, the freedom of the citizens sharing social welfare in the forms of justice and enjoying rights to participate in politics, must be safeguarded. This kind of right of freedom is an expression of the subjects' active initiatives. It can be called as freedom of active initiatives. Plato holds that an ideal nation is a just nation. Justice contains all most basic virtues of the human beings. The goal of his "justice in the city-state" theory is to maintain orders in the city-state and the harmony among various strata. Aristotle regards justice as important means to adjust social political life, to ease social conflicts and to maintain social stability, deeming that justice is just the general name of various virtues. Hume pointed out: "The public efficiency is the only origin of justice." John Rawls claims in his book *The Theory of Justice*: "Justice is the primary value of social systems." The justice-principle stresses that, various kinds of basic rights and responsibilities must be evenly distributed. At the same time, the interests and burdens resulted from social cooperation should be distributed as evenly as possible. He holds that various posts and positions should be open to all people equally. He also deems: "The social justice principle's main problem is the society's basic structure, and is a kind of main social systematic array in the cooperation system", making justice and fairness obtain certain arrangement in the system. Only by doing this, can it be possible to further establish a set of justice norms and ethics which is universally reasonable and effective. Justice of a system consists of two aspects, namely the justice of the system itself and the justice of the operation of the system. The purpose of the systematic justice is just for safeguarding fairness of interests and adjusting well the interest conflicts between collectives and individuals.

Therefore, a just society, on the one hand, needs to appropriately handle the issue of competition fairness and exchange fairness in social activities, and on the other hand, it needs to properly handle the relationship between the public interests and the private interests, especially emphasizing that government officials cannot illegally trespass public interests or abuse government power to pursue private interests. We cannot allow a few people or some small interest groups to trespass public interests in the name of "the collective". A just society enables all citizens to have a sense of ownership, making joint efforts to safeguard the orders and stability of the social life. "Justice is obviously conducive to promoting public efficacy and to supporting a civilized society. Only when justice has become a virtue, and various parts and various factors in the social system are at a state of mutual coordination, can the society become a harmonious society".

A harmonious society, as a state of social progress, advocates active and benign interaction between collectives and individuals, protecting the subjects' freedom of creativity. A harmonious society provides a unique perspective for human freedom, and meanwhile provides directions for theory of practical ethics: seeking ways of transition from the human state of being slaved to the state of freedom. A harmonious society should be a society of the rational and free human beings, in which the individuals' rational capacities have full play, the individuals' enthusiasm and subjective initiatives in subject activities unprecedentedly increase, the spaces for the individuals' free actions are extremely expanded, and the whole society is full of vigor and vitality. In a harmonious society, each individual equally and fully enjoys individual freedom in legality and formality. Furthermore, the individuals can use such freedom to pursue their happiness and create wonderful life. At an even higher level, a harmonious society affirms human survival, human dignity, human happiness and living conditions in conformity with humanity, thus enabling people to achieve spiritual freedom and enabling people's temperament harmony to realize the settlement of mind orders.

C. *Discrimination and an Analysis of Freedom Limits Related To Issues between Collectives and Individuals.* "Freedom" is the core of the whole Western liberalist current of thought. What is freedom? There is only one true freedom, which is to pursue personal interests with one's own approaches. Moreover, such pursuit does not deprive of others' interests nor hinder others' efforts in pursuing their interests. A harmonious society is one of pluralism where subjects enjoy ample freedom. Pluralism cannot reject authorities; nor does it mean abuse of freedom.

First, *the rights in the private domain are the most basic human rights.* On the one hand, the public domain cannot violate the private domain. Due to the special nature of the relationship between people and the power systems, excessive private factors have penetrated the power of the public domain, fundamentally preventing the safeguarding of citizens' rights. On the other hand, the rights of the private domain cannot harm each other. In other words, the obtaining of a private right cannot hinder or violate that of other people. For example, free speech is a right in private domain, but free speech that spreads slanders, frames a case against other people, or threatens other people's lives must be forbidden. In a civilized and progressive society with a good conscientious legal system, whatever is not vested legally the public power does not have the right to "self-judge," and whatever is not forbidden legally in the domain of private activities the public power does not have the power to intervene. Only in a society in which citizens enjoy ample freedom in private domains and public and private domains are distinctive and supportive of each other do we find harmony and happiness.

Second, *the demarcations between "individual domains" and "collective domains" are not always fixed.* For example, in the movie *Titanic*, the right to survival, a most basic, private right, is also handled as an issue in the public domain. Another example is citizens' childbearing rights, an issue in the private domain. But under the severe situation of overpopulation in China, the choice of family planning, which is not the best yet not the worst measure," is in conformity with the development interests of the collectives and the nation. In this case, "the unlimitedness of private desires and the people's setting of limits for the private domain for the sake of their own fundamental interests in the public domain does not form a contradiction.

Third, *there is a correlation between collectives and individuals.* There is a distinction between "the false collective" and "the true collective." Under the condition of a true collective, each individual obtains his or her freedom in and through his or her union. The "true collective" is the union of various free laborers. Each individual obtains freedom from this kind of union. Under the condition of socialism, the collective principle is the spiritual motive promoting social justice, morality, and justice; it is the way to guarantee that people are able to realize their values, the practical way to promote people's free and all-around development, and the reliable political safeguard that ensures that the people are masters of the nation and enjoy widespread democracy.

- First, we need to start trying to understand both people and society. In other words we need to start from the "true individual" to understand the society.

- Second, we need to, on the basis of dialectical methodology, scientifically solve the relationship between people's personal character and sociality. The more sociality in human activities, the more independence people have. Human beings "are not only a kind of sociable animals, furthermore, only when being in the society can they be independent animals."

- Third, we need to correctly handle the relationship between individuals and unity. The full development of individuals can only be realized in a collective, while the existence and development of a collective can only be realized through the existence and development of individuals. At the same time, freedom must be vested to the individuals. Free individuals whose characters are constructed on the basis of personal all-around development and the understanding that their common social forms have become their social wealth are the third stage of human social development. Only at this stage, as a complete human being, does one possess his or her overall essence. At this time, the free development of every person is the condition of each individual's free development. When we discuss the relationship between the collective and the individual, we need to be individual-oriented while discarding the modern radical individualism, eliminating confrontation among individuals, and establishing a holistic and equal human-to-human relationship. Very obviously, when it comes to harmony between collectives and individuals, limiting individualism is necessary. Some postmodern thinkers also understand that individualism has already become origins of various problems in the modern society.

In general, a harmonious society is characterized by freedom with limits and by abundant creativities; in such a society, conflicts among social members are infrequent and mutual respect between collective and individual domains exists. Social development must be human-oriented, aptly coordinating the relationship between overall social interests and individual interests; creating a good social atmosphere, a harmonious interpersonal environment, and a social order that incorporates harmony with differences; and stimulating the vitality of the whole society. We believe that a society with harmony between collectives and individuals is an ever-flourishing society.

Harmony among Ethnic Groups Promotes National Rejuvenation

Around 2,000 ethnic groups currently live on this planet. This diversity informs various aspects of social life, such as politics, economy, culture, and international relations, spanning across both horizontal and vertical connections, which cross and penetrate each other. To solve the issues of discord among ethnic groups is a long-term historic process. It's not possible to eliminate an ethnic group through compulsory assimilation, through violent or administrative means; these means, rather, render ethnic problems even more acute. To artificially complete the melting process of ethnic groups is also against the law and would not possibly solve ethnic group issues. Only by enabling various ethnic groups to fully develop will there be conscious amalgamation. It is possible that a natural withering away of definitive lines between the groups would result from such amalgamation. And these are simply the supreme manifestations of the Culture of Harmony. While emphasizing common development among all human beings, we respect the differences among ethnic groups. *Harmony with differences* is the ultimate key to solving problems between ethnic groups. We must constantly seek balance in the unbalanced social development process, so as to make benefits available to various ethnic groups.

We live in a world with many ethnic groups (over two thousand) and pluralism in over two hundred countries. Except for a very small number of countries, basically every country is home to multiple ethnic groups. It would be very difficult to say that any country does not have any ethnic problems. These are universal issues. Generally speaking, there are the following types of ethnic problems in the current world, according to the division of regions:

We can find the first type of ethnic group problems in the former USSR and some Eastern European countries, where ethnic groups split and the countries dismembered. The former USSR, founded on December 30, 1922, was composed of four allied Soviet Democratic Republics—the Russian Federation, the South Caucasus Federation, Ukraine, and Belarus. These former allied republics were basically named according to the dominant ethnic group. Between 1924 and1940, the number of allied republics in the former USSR increased to sixteen. From the mid-1950s until the dissolution of the former USSR in 1991, there were fifteen allied republics. They jointly formed the former USSR. The former USSR existed for nearly seventy years before its dissolution under the rule of Mikhail Sergeyevich Gorbachev. The fifteen allied republics resumed their original names. Why was the former USSR dissolved? The poor handling of the issues between ethnic groups was an important cause.

In other Eastern European countries, for example in the former Yugoslavia, the former unified Yugoslavia was dissolved into five countries from one federal republic. Later, Bosnia's Serbians, Muslims, and Croatians experienced years of war; hundreds of thousands died, and millions became refugees. Especially in the region of Kosovo in 1999, ethnic group conflicts and hatred between the Albanians and the Serbians reached an unprecedented level. A few ethnic group extremists, with the support of foreign forces, formed the Albanian Liberation Army and fought against the Yugoslavian government, finally causing the people of various ethnic groups in Kosovo the tremendous scourge of war.

We find the second type of ethnic conflicts in African countries. As former colonies of Western countries, the relatively weak and small countries of Africa suffer because of the history of colonial rule and its companion, slavery. After colonial rule came to an end, although the people of the former colonies achieved national independence and national liberation, the hidden troubles and roots of discord left by the colonial rule were not uprooted. The seeds of hatred between ethnic groups sown by the colonial rule resulted in frequent conflicts between ethnic groups and clans. This was prominent in the conflicts and vengeful murders between the Hutu and the Tutsis in Rwanda. During the blood-shedding of the 1990s, the number of deaths caused by clan conflicts in Rwanda reached millions. The frequent conflicts between clans and ethnic groups in African countries have caused serious refugee problems. According to the statistics of the United Nations Refugee Agency, the number of refugees increased from 15 million in 1990 to 23 million in 2000. This increase of more than 7 million is the equivalent of the population of a medium-sized country. Of the 23 million refugees, 11.8 million were in Africa, among whom 2 million Rwanda refugees fled to other countries, and another 2 million became destitute and homeless. In the small country of Burundi, more than 800,000 people became refugees, and more than a million more became homeless. In Mozambique, 2.9 million people became homeless and more than a million fled to other countries. These are the tragedies caused by ethnic group conflicts and vengeful clan murders; such actions are very incompatible with the development of human civilization.

We find a third type of ethnic conflict in the Middle East, where Arabic and Israeli ethnic groups are at odds. The problems in the Middle East are mainly the result of conflicts and contradictions among Arabs who believe in Islamism and Israelis who believe in Judaism. These conflicts and contradictions are still very far from ending. Water resources, land, immigration issues, the establishment of the Palestinian state, and the status of Jerusalem are the primary sources of conflict between these two large ethnic groups. Israel currently has a population of six million people, among whom five million are Jews and a million are Arabic. During World War II, Nazi Germany tried its utmost to eliminate the Jewish ethnic group. The Jews not only survived the massacre but, rather, increased in population. The number of Jewish people in the United States is greater than that in the Israeli homeland. Many play roles in the US high society, and some hold important bureaucratic positions.

We find the fourth type of ethnic dispute in countries that practice policies of ethnic or racial discrimination. Western countries have followed a twisted path with three basic phases.

During the first phase, Western countries practiced policies that enabled the bloody massacre of ethnic groups, mainly in the early stage of capitalist development. The Enclosure Movement practiced early on in capitalist countries expelled the indigenous ethnic groups, even killing many of them, just as was done to the indigenous ethnic groups in the colonies in the past. This kind of policy that led to massacres, on the one hand, caused international opposition and, on the other hand, intensified ethnic conflicts. It is impossible to eliminate ethnic groups. A better approach would be to seek methods for easing rather than intensifying the conflicts.

During the second phase, these countries adopted policies of preservation. After capitalism took political power, in order to ease the social contradictions, the governments designated certain pieces of land as reservations for the indigenous ethnic groups, allowed them to develop production, and even gave them certain help. But these policies did not let indigenous populations contact other ethnic groups. They were enclosed. Finally, these indigenous ethnic groups can only lead their lives in exclusion. This is actually a kind of ethnic discrimination policy.

In the third phase, Western countries adopted a kind of multicultural policy. As time moved on and ethnic groups awakened, some Western countries began to adjust their policies. For example,

Canada and some other countries—in order to maintain their own rule and international image—began to adjust their ethnic policies so as to ease conflicts among ethnic groups. As a result, these countries now practice a relatively popular policy—the so-called multicultural policy. Compared with former policies, this policy has made relatively great progress. Comparatively, it conforms to the needs of the current multifaceted, multielemented, and multiethnic society. This is a new model for handling relationships between ethnic groups.

In addition, to the four types of the ethnic conflicts mentioned about, those found in countries such as India, Sri Lanka, Indonesia, and Turkey are relatively acute. But these contradictions and conflicts are basically regional, not having important impacts on peace and development of the whole world, and thus not being included in the above-mentioned four types.

We can point to five major contributors to these four basic categories of ethnic conflicts in the current world.

A. The accumulated resentment and problems left by a *history of colonial rule* are the root causes for many current world ethnic problems.

B. The end of the Cold War provided opportunities for ethnic conflicts to break out, as a result of the *former contention for world hegemony.*

C. *Misguided formulation and implementation of ethnic group policies* in various countries are practical, inherent contributors to current ethnic problems.

D. *Hegemonic policies and power politics* are the international political root causes of a host of current world ethnic problems.

E. *Economic globalization and contradictions between developed countries, less developed countries, and third-world countries* are international, economic root causes to ethnic conflicts.

The world's people need peace and development. With peace, the links among various countries and ethnic groups in the world would be even closer. Interdependence would gradually deepen. Various ethnic groups must participate in the developmental processes of the countries in which they live. They must do so with an attitude that embraces equality and tolerance; seeks to understand other ethnic groups' faith and culture; and focuses on self-respect, self-confidence, and the desire to become stronger. The future development of the world's ethnic groups can only take the steady road of "Harmony with differences" under the prerequisite of practical international basic principles that forward this goal.

HARMONY AMONG RELIGIONS PROMOTES WORLD PEACE

Religion is a kind of cultural phenomenon that emerged when human society had developed to a certain stage. Being a social ideology, its main characteristic is a belief in a supernatural, mysterious power or substance that exists outside of the practical world, commands all things under the sun, and possesses absolute authority. It controls the evolution of nature and decides the destiny of the human world, thus inspiring awe, veneration, and worship in people. This veneration extends to cognitive beliefs and ritual activities.

In some early human social formations, religions assumed functions like explaining the world, judicial judgment, ethical cultivation, and psychological consolation. In the modern society, scientific and judiciary roles have been separated from some religions, but many people still rely on religion for ethical cultivation and psychological consolation. The belief systems and social communities that religions form are an important component of human ideology, culture, and social formations.

The human history is a history of culture. The history of ethnic groups is also a history of culture. And the origin of culture can be traced back to ancient religious culture. Therefore, undoubtedly, religious cultures should also become important resources for our construction of Harmony today. Religion is a cultural phenomenon, and yet it is a cultural phenomenon that manifests spiritual belief. The disharmony of the whole world and society and the driving of and vying for economic benefits and resource occupation rates are definitely profound reasons for disharmony in the world. However, conflicts between different religions and the civilizations that inherited these religions are a source of disharmony that must face squarely. A unique characteristic of religious beliefs is their locality. At the same time, sometimes religions arise in situations of exclusiveness.

In society, a certain number of ethnic groups and religious believers from different religions form groups. Under the flag of shared religious beliefs, they, over long periods of time, maintain their own independent beliefs while living in different regions and communities. Thus we have situations in which a particular religion crosses national and community boundaries, having both regions of large and small concentrations. However, due to historic differences and because religions are generally local and exclusive in nature, ethnic groups and believer groups from different religions often have various kinds of clashes of thoughts and conflicts of actions.

In the past century, the conflicts of different religions and gang fighting with weapons among clans have been troubling some countries continuously, seriously hindering these countries' socioeconomic development. The features of a harmonious society include a peaceful and friendly atmosphere everywhere, respect and understanding between the various ethnic communities, equality for all, and an absence of disputes. Various countries and various communities are founded under systems of equality and order, in which the cultures of traditional ethnic groups and diverse religious beliefs are fully praised and everyone's mind is at ease.

Judging from this, in order to build harmonious societies (and, thus, a harmonious world), religions' roles must include maintaining harmony in believers' minds, eliminating covetous desires, and resolving brutality. Each religion should start with itself and change from exclusive competition into tolerant coexistence. Thus, we will achieve harmony inside the religions and among the religions. Only when we have religious harmony can we have harmony among ethnic groups and realize harmony in our societies and our world. Human beings have their own limitations. In order to overcome these limitations, they created religions. As things created and controlled by human beings, specific religions may possibly have their limitations.

To pursue religious harmony is a condition of religions playing an active role in promoting social harmony and also an opportunity for religions to attempt to break their limitations. Religions' self-restraints when it comes to conducting ethnical cultivation and psychological consolation have formed a commonality of the religions. That is the commonality that Harmony pursues. But different religions have different forms, and this is "Harmony with Differences."

Harmony among Nations Builds World Peace

In order to enable nations to respect each other's sovereignty and territorial integrity, we must not invade each other or interfere in each other's internal affairs. Rather we must exercise practices that emphasize equality and mutual benefit. The world's nations must politically respect each other, discuss related issues, and refrain from imposing one's own will on others. Economically, they should promote each other, prioritizing common development and avoiding the creation of huge gaps between the rich and the poor. Culturally, they should learn from each other, with a focus on achieving common prosperity but should not reject other ethnic cultures. In security affairs, they should trust each other; make joint efforts to maintain security; establish a new security outlook of mutual trust, mutual benefit, equality, and cooperation; and settle their disputes through dialogue and cooperation. They should not use violence or the threat of violence. These methods would truly create world peace. The relationships between nations must be based on in-depth studies of the relationships between ethnic groups and nations.

Ethnic groups and nations are historic phenomena that arose from different stages of the development of human society. They are all in the historic domain. There exist both commonalities and great differences between the two. Ethnic groups and nations are twins, who were born together, rely on each other, exist together, and interactively develop together. The relationship between the two is close and complicated. They promote each other and affect each other. Correctly understanding the commonalities and differences of ethnic groups and nations and their relationships, properly handling the interests and claims of ethnic groups and nations, and engaging with multiple ethnic groups—these measures are all conducive to harmony, stability, unity, and development.

A. *Differences and Commonalities between Ethnic Groups and Nations.* Both ethnic groups and nations are historic phenomena that emerged at certain stages in the development of human society. Ethnic groups are steady human unions with basic distinctive features formed in human history. Nations, on the other hand, are products and expressions of the disharmony of class contradictions—machines safeguarding the rules of certain classes over other classes and agencies by which economically ruling classes conduct class rule and administer public affairs of a society as a whole. Ethnic groups and nations have natural and extremely close links. In some countries in the West, the concepts of ethnic groups and nations, in many occasions, are interchangeable. In English, the three words *nation*, *state*, and *country* can all be translated into the same two Chinese characters, "国家", but they have different focuses. *Nation* refers to a country formed by people, *state* refers to a country from the angle of the government, and *country* mainly refers to a geographic region defined by certain boundaries. Here, the people referred to by the word *nation* are the unions who form ethnic groups. Therefore, in English, nation has two meanings—"ethnic group" and "country." Nations in The United Nations also means "country." We can say that the words *ethnic group* and *nation* mean the same thing, as ethnic groups form nations. This is true not only for single-ethnic countries but also for nations that are home to multiple ethnic groups.

The common points of ethnic groups and nations are not limited to this. Both ethnic groups and nations are unions of human groups and were formed at the end of primitive societies when class-based societies emerged.

Furthermore, both ethnic groups and regions developed on the basis of common regions. Especially in single-ethnic countries, the basic features of ethnic groups and certain characteristics of nations are the same. For example, the language the ethnic group uses is also that of the nation. Similarly, the common region of the ethnic group is also the range of the nation's territory. The economic life of the ethnic group is also the nation's economic life. The mentality of the ethnic group is also the mentality of the nationals of the nation. In single-ethnic nations, generally speaking, the members of the ethnic nationals that comprise the country are one and the same. When people talk about an ethnic group, they refer to the nation; when people talk about a nation, they refer to the ethnic group. Perhaps because of this, *nation* can be used to mean both "country" and "ethnic group" in English.

However, there were very great differences between ethnic groups and nations during the courses of their formation and development. First of all, although both are unions of human groups, *the basic factors of the formation of ethnic groups and nations are not the same*. Generally speaking, ethnic groups share four basic features that together result in a common mentality—common geographical regions, common languages, common economic lives, and common cultures. The basic factors for forming nations, on the other hand, are as follows:

- *Populations or certain numbers of residents or ethnic groups who have settled down in specific countries and specific regions.* Such groups are the first basic factor for forming nations and the foundation on which all activities of nations are predicated.
- *Territories or places where residents live and rest or the common geographical regions of ethnic groups.* In multiethnic nations, this is the sum of the common geographic regions of ethnic groups. These are the spaces in which states practice their power and providers of the material foundations on which nations rely in order to survive.

- *Sovereignty, or the united and inseparable, supreme power to handle one's own internal and external affairs.* These are fundamental attributes of a nation.
- *Governments, or the highest administrative organs of nations.* A governing body is the most important part of a state and its most important tool for realizing its rules and dictatorship.

Of course, besides these basic factors, states, as products of class societies, are definitely founded on the basis of certain social, economic, and class relationships.

Second, although both are social and political entities, *ethnic groups and nations have different focuses.* Ethnic groups have endured as human groups forming political units while nations have endured as political mechanisms. In ethnic groups, factors like economy, culture (including outlooks), languages, and regions link people. Ethnic groups have their own interest principles and value orientations. States, on the other hand, are tools of class rule, with a full ruling body and definite territories and nationals under their rule. In states, political motivations are the main forces that link people in conformity to political interests. States mainly rely on their political mechanism to adjust the relationships among various classes, social groups, and ethnic groups, so as to safeguard the stability and order of their rule. To judge these two kinds of entities, states have deeper political colors while ethnic groups have deeper cultural colors.

Third, *the stabilities of ethnic groups and countries are different.* Once an ethnic group is formed, it possesses relative stability. It would not immediately change with political commotion or change of territory. A country, on the other hand, would immediately change due to reasons such as political commotion, change of territory, conflicts between ethnic groups, and foreign invasion. For example, the former USSR, having been founded more than seventy years earlier, collapsed like a huge building without a solid foundation, due to intensifying conflicts, such as those in the fields of history, ethnic groups, politics, and economy. The nation fell, splitting into a good number of new nations of ethnic groups. But the various ethnic groups in the former USSR, as ethnic unions, still remained unchanged, although some ethnic groups respectively changed to belong to several different countries.

Fourth, *both ethnic groups and countries are divided by regions, but there are differences between these regions.* A common region of an ethnic group is the material foundation on which the ethnic group survives and develops; a common region is one of the most important conditions for the forming of an ethnic group. However in multiethnic countries, the regions of ethnic groups are simply parts of the country's territory. Furthermore, once an ethnic group is formed, a common region is not an indispensable feature of the group. With migration of ethnic groups and strengthening of ethnic contacts, the cohabitation of various ethnic groups in certain regions will increase. For example, in China a feature of the distribution of ethnic groups is that different ethnic groups cohabitate in vast areas, while in some small areas, one ethnic group or another is highly concentrated. States, on the other hand enjoy absolute sovereignty over their specific territories, not allowing any other states to share with them.

Fifth, *a common language is a feature of and an important factor in the formation of an ethnic group, whereas a nation does not necessarily need a common language.* For example, in Switzerland, three languages—German, French, and Italian—are all official languages. In a multiethnic country, although one language or several languages serve as the country's official language(s), other ethnic languages still exist.

Sixth, *common economic life is the decisive condition for the formation and development of an ethnic group.* Without common economic life, it is not possible for an ethnic group to form. If various parts of an ethnic group are separated from each other economically for a long period of time, different changes will occur in the various factions of the ethnic group; a faction will be assimilated by another ethnic group; or just as some English people who moved to North America did, a faction will form a new ethnic group. In the economic life of countries, varied and diversified economic characteristics exist due to factors such as the differences among various ethnic groups and natural geographical and climatic features.

Seventh, *common mentality is an indispensable spiritual factor in forming an ethnic group.* An ethnic group is different from other ethnic groups not only because its material living conditions are different but also because the spiritual formations expressed in its cultural characteristics are different. Of course, an ethnic group's common mentality will not always remain the same. It is a reflection of this group's material living conditions and will change as the ethnic group's living conditions change. But the nature of the relative independence of spiritual culture ensures that an ethnic group's common mentality develops on its own tracks, has a relatively strong inheritance and stable nature, and is firmly tied to maintaining the group's existence and injecting active and lasting vital power into its survival and development. Thus, the spiritual culture becomes the most lasting and most staunching component part of the ethnic group's various characteristics. In contrast, in a multiethnic country, as the ethnic groups are different, their cultures will also inevitably display pluralism; the ethnic groups' mentalities expressed in various cultural characteristics would also inevitably be diverse, often with great differences.

B. *Relationship between Ethnic Groups and Nations.* An ethnic group and a nation are a pair of twin entities who are born together and rely on each other for survival and interactive development. In the course of the formation of an ethnic group, the nation plays the role of facilitator, whereas ethnic groups are important bases for a nation's structure and development. The relationship between them is extremely close and complex. They promote each other and influence each other.

Ethnic Groups Are *One of the Important Factors for Determining the Structural Forms of States.* The structural form of a state refers to the nature and pattern of the mutual relationship between the state's central political power and the local political powers and to the mutual relationship between the state's overall integrity and all its integral parts. We might also refer to this as a state's system. According to the different relationships between the central organization and the local organizations, the state's structural forms are mainly divided into two forms—the unitary-system state and the composite-system state. Furthermore, the composite states include two forms—the federal states and the confederated states. A state, whether its structure and development are unitary or whether it's comprised of a multiethnic group, is directly related to ethnic groups. Because of that, in certain stages of social development, the population of a nation belongs to certain ethnic groups. Members of ethnic groups are, at the same time, members of a nation. Therefore, ethnic groups are the basis of a nation's survival and development. Especially in modern times, the ethnic groups in a multiethnic group nation and the mutual relationship between them are important factors for decisions within the political system about the state's structural form and degree of political stability and whether or not the state is united or split. A single-ethnic state normally establishes a unitary system state, while a multiethnic state normally establishes a federal state. For example, France, Italy, Japan, Norway, and Sweden are unitary-system states, while the United States, Germany, Switzerland, Canada, and Brazil have adopted the federal system. The establishments and developments of the federal system in these countries are varied from each other.

China is a multiethnic country that has not adopted the federal system, choosing a unitary structural form instead. This was also a decision based on ethnic characteristics, historic traditions, and the characteristics of the social system. China is home to various ethnic groups who cohabitate; the Han ethnicity is the main body. The Han comprises about 94 percent of the nation's total population. Since various ethnic groups' development in politics, economy, and culture is imbalanced, a unified unitary system is favorable, as it concentrates superiorities in order to speed up progress in categories such as cutting-edge development and ethnic issues. In the fields of resources, personnel, managerial experience, and economic development level, ethnic groups may better draw on the strengths of others to make up for their weaknesses, so as to achieve common developmental prosperity. While adopting the unitary system, China also fully takes into consideration various ethnic characteristics. Thus the nation establishes corresponding autonomous organizations among various minority ethnic groups that inhabited certain areas in high concentration. This allows the ethnic groups to practice autonomy, thus guaranteeing the state's solidarity and unity, and also better solving ethnic problems.

The Relationship of Interdependence and Interactive Development of Both Ethnic Groups and States. Ethnic groups and states were born together and are interdependent. Especially in modern times, the state becomes an important political carrier on which ethnic groups rely for survival development. There are fewer and fewer ethnic groups are not attached to any formations of states. Ethnic who remain autonomous generally either suffer fates (like that of the Kurds) or naturally, silently gradually disappear in the vast sea of ethnic groups world (like the Gypsies). Fates of ethnic groups linked with the fate of a state. If a state is strong groups thrive. If a state is weak, its ethnic groups the role that the state plays in promoting the d its ethnic groups is very important and can by any other social forces. A state's roles and be manifested in three aspects:

- First, *the state provides an external environment that is favorable for the development of ethnic groups.* The state establishes good international relationships by making, adjusting, and implementing diplomatic policies, so as to provide a relatively peaceful and stable international environment for the ethnic groups' development. This allows ethnic groups to be productive and lead their lives and facilitates international contacts and cooperation among various ethnic groups, opening up international markets and other global interactions. The state can also provide a good internal environment for an ethnic group's development—principally, a good political environment, a good foundation for ethnic relations and developmental opportunities.

As to the political environment, states' political activities, such as the national constitution; special laws; and principles, policies, and measures—both of the central government and the local governments—provide ethnic groups autonomy at various levels.

States also provide for good ethnic relations—social relationships involving members of ethnic groups. In the course of an ethnic groups' survival and development, issues arising from relationships between ethnic groups often occur in various aspects of social life, such as politics, economy, culture, education, lifestyles and religious beliefs. To coordinate such relationships, the states' legal, administrative, educational, and compulsory means are necessary. When ethnic group relationships are well coordinated, they promote not just the ethnic group's development but that of the state as well.

The state provides the ethnic groups with developmental opportunities. The social and economic developments of an ethnic group are the premise of its developments in other fields. Although we cannot deny the important roles of politics, culture, and education, in the final analysis, the degree to which an ethnic group develops is decided by its social and economic progress.

- Second, *the state can adjust the internal mechanism for promoting an ethnic group's development.* The state's functions in this field are mainly manifested as the coordination, promotion, and optimization of an ethnic group's internal structure. The components of an ethnic group's structure include economic, political, cultural, ideological, population, and family structures. In a well-coordinated ethnic group, one that finds itself in a good cycle, the relationships between the various components of its structure are the driving force for the group's development. On the contrary, if the ethnic group's internal structure is not rational or irregular, the relationships between its components will generate a great impeding force, weakening the group's already not-so-powerful drive and resulting in a slow or even stagnate state of the ethnic group's development. The state's important role in promoting an ethnic group's own development is that of adjusting the group's structures—making them rational and optimized. For example, when an ethnic group's educational structure is not compatible with its economic structure, this hampers not only its educational development but also its economic development. If its economy is not developed, the ethnic group cannot put more into its education, and its educational lack will remain an issue. In this case, it's necessary for the state to promote the development of the ethnic group's educational system through policy intervention and funding, so as to gradually suit and promote the group's economic development.

- Third, *the state plays an important role in improving the quality of the ethnic group*. Ethnic groups' qualities vary due to the differences in their historical developments and degrees of growth. Ethnic group quality is a comprehensive index for measuring the degree of an ethnic group's development. The state plays an important role in improving an ethnic group's quality and promoting its development. Changing and improving an existing ethnic group's quality enables the ethnic group to develop under new conditions, with new starting points, and at a higher rate.

In summary, the state provides a number of critical conditions, policies, and measures that are indispensable to the ethnic group's development. With the powerful support and help of the state, an ethnic group's political, economic, and cultural development will improve, along with its population quality and social life. In addition, the relationships among various ethnic groups will be better coordinated and more harmonious. Moreover, the continuous strengthening of ethnic groups' solidarity will, in turn, invaluably promote the state's various developmental undertakings. Strong, solid ethnic groups will strengthen the comprehensive national strength and the state's unity and prosperity. Therefore, ethnic groups and the states in which they live are interdependent and interactive. They must develop together.

A correct understanding of the differences, commonalities, and relationships between ethnic groups and states—and an understanding of how to properly handle the interests and claims of each—will promote harmony, stability, unity, and development in multiethnic group countries.

To summarize the above-mentioned points, in practice, Harmony is manifested in kind hearts, families in concord, solving contradictions, a harmonious society, a peaceful world, and a happy future. All things in the universe can coexist peacefully without any mutual violation.

Harmony as the Unity of the World Outlook and Methodology

THE DIALECTICAL RELATIONSHIP OF SEEKING COMMONALITIES WHILE RESERVING DIFFERENCES

To "seek commonalities" means to search for universally applicable principles that apply to human beings' understanding and transformation of the world. To "reserving differences" is to research the differences among people's processes of understanding and transforming the world. In this complex world, we must command universally applicable principles while, at the same time, peeling away the nature of differences and gradually realizing the unity of both commonalities and differences. This process of unity is the process of seeking commonalities. All things have universally applicable principles—an existing universally objective law. But simply understanding universally applicable principles is not the same as truly understanding the essence of things. Only when we have peeled away these universalities (commonalities) and found the differences of a thing have we found its special nature; only then can we truly understand its essence. Understanding the commonalities of things and peeling them away to discover the differences comprise the process of "seeking commonalities while reserving the differences." The human processes of understanding and transforming the world contain both "seeking major commonalities while reserving minor differences" and "seeking minor commonalities while reserving major differences."

A. *Seeking Major Commonalities While Reserving Minor Differences.* What do we mean by "seeking" when we say "seeking for major commonalities"? The "seeking" is a kind of exploration, a search to ascertain of objective determinations about the process of development.

When people try to understand a subject or solve a contradiction, they must first determine the nature of the matter and what kind of problems are to be solved. "Seeking major commonalities" is also the first premise for understanding and solving whatever problem is at hand. To "seek major commonalities" is to search complicated concepts or objects for common features in order to solve and understand problems. Only when we have determined the common features can we understand the commonality of a concept or object. For example, if we are to cultivate and care for a pot of flowers, first we need to seek its "major commonalities"—we must determine whether it is a plant or an animal. Since the flowers are a type of plants and possess characteristics common to plants, we know that we need to water the flowers but not feed it like we would if we were caring for an animal.

By determining the common characteristics of plants we solve the problem of how to care for the flowers.

Therefore, "seeking major commonalities" is the premise for understanding and solving the problem.

"Reserving in "reserving minor differences" refers to maintaining the ability to identify differences. There exist differences between things with common characteristics and between any two otherwise identical objects. To reserve "minor differences," we must identify the differences in the commonalities. This is a fundamental law for handling problems and solving problems. When we cultivate flowers, we must notice that all flowers possess the characteristics common to plants. To determine how we can best help specific flowers grow sturdily, we must conduct research on the differences among varieties of plants. Sunflowers like sunshine, while night *Telosma cordata* (Chinese violet) only blossoms at night. Therefore, when seeking for major commonalities while reserving minor differences, we need to search for common characteristics and, more importantly, we must find the differences within common groups. Only when we organically unify the nature of both the commonalities and differences of an object or concept can we truly handle it well. The process of organically unifying these commonalities and differences of things is the process of seeking commonalities while reserving differences; it is the process of pursuing Harmony. This is why we must understand and solve problems.

We can apply this reasoning to other problems. For example, to solve various problems that the modern international community is facing, we also need to apply a process of "seeking major commonalities while reserving minor differences." This includes:

- *Political issues,* such as nuclear proliferation, regional wars, antiterrorism, poverty among countries, ethnic conflicts

- *Economic issues,* such as the financial crisis, problems with the foreign exchange rate, international economic relations, shortage of consumption demand in developing countries, the rising cost of energy, grain security, and the increasing pressure of global inflation

- *Cultural issues.* When United States President Barack Obama visited China in November 2009, in his dialogue with Shanghai youngsters, he said:

> One of American superiorities is that we have a much diversified culture. There we have people come from various parts of the world. So, what do Americans look like? You really cannot answer this question in a simple word. For example, in my family, my father came from Kenya, my mother came from the Kansas State in the central western part of the US. My younger sister is a half-Indonesian and she married a Canadian Chinese. So when you see the Obama family gathering, we look like being in the United Nations where you can see all kinds of people. This is where the US strength comes from. Because it means that we can learn from each other's different cultures, different food and different thoughts. This makes our society more vigorous. At the same time, each country lives in a world having other countries. Among you, you have me. Among us, we have you. Each country has

its own historic tradition and culture. So I think, for the US, one important point is that, we cannot say that whatever works for us would also work for others, and would be beneficial to others. Actually, in this aspect, we should be modest, we should have modest attitude towards other countries.

- *Natural ecological issues*, such as global warming, ozone layer damage, acid rain, the freshwater resource crisis, energy shortage, sharply decreased forest resources, soil degradation, accelerated extinction of species, trash overflow, and air pollution due to poisonous chemicals, all of which are environmental issues that threaten humanity's survival.

The London Exhibition Hall in the 2010 World Expo was called "Zero Carbon Hall". It advises people to lead low-carbon lifestyles. In other words, it proposes that we should do our utmost to reduce the amount of energy that we consume during our daily lives, so as to reduce the emission of carbon dioxide. Low-carbon lifestyles, where ordinary people are concerned, are a kind of attitude not a capability. We should actively advocate and practice a low-carbon lifestyle by paying attention to ways we can save electricity, gasoline, and natural gas as much as possible. Besides planting trees, some people buy products manufactured locally or use stairs instead of elevators. People save energy in a great variety of ways. Some activities are very easy while some are executed with a little more trouble. Those who are concerned about global warming seek practical methods of reducing carbon dioxide emissions in their daily lives.

- *World peace and development issues.* Peace and development are major subjects of the current era. Peace issue is a political issue. Development is an economic issue. Therefore, the relationship between peace and development may manifest as follows: Peace is the premise and basis of development. Only in a peaceful international environment can the various countries of the world maintain normal economic contacts and smoothly realize their national development plans. The world economic development after World War II benefited from the relatively stable international environment. Wars and conflicts are obstacles of economic development. Wars not only force participating countries to consume huge amounts of labor forces, materials, and financial resources, causing serious economic losses, they also paralyze communications and transportation and interrupt international trade, seriously influencing the development of world economy.

Developing the economy is a powerful guarantee of safeguarding world peace. Peace needs a certain material basis, whereas the economic and trade contacts can promote friendly contacts between people in various countries. Specifically, the development of world economy promotes international labor division and increases the exchange and unity among various countries, possibly curbing the breakout of a world war. Economic development is conducive to eliminating unstable factors in the world and to reducing the possibilities of military conflicts. The development of world economy, especially among developing countries, is conducive to strengthening the force of world peace.

Thus, we can see that peace and development are mutually conditional, interrelated, and interacting.

B. *Seeking Minor Commonalities while Reserving Major Differences.* To "seeking minor commonalities" is to realize the universality and commonality of contradiction through the particularities of the contradiction. Skillful discovery of the particularities of contradictions—of the commonalities within the particularities—and analysis of each distinct, concrete problem distinctively is a magic weapon; it is the pith and marrow in solving contradictions and problems. The old saying about "knowing the whole leopard through one spot" explains why. Judging from a sociological point of view and from the angle of people's behavioral ethics and interpersonal relationship, we should do our best to discover other people's merits and handle our interpersonal relationship based on these merits. Then our interpersonal relationships will become more harmonious.

C. *Realizing Humankind's Bright Future: Clearing up the Universe with a Gentle Breeze.* Realizing humankind's bright future thusly is the sum of the spiritual results human beings achieve in the course of their transformation of the objective and subjective world and a progressive state of human wisdom and ethics. Behavior that manifests in a clearing up of the universe can be categorized in two fields. The first is the field of science and culture, including the situation of culture, knowledge and wisdom in the society, and the development scales and levels of undertakings like education, science, culture, arts, hygiene, and sports. The second is the field of ideology and morality, including political ideology, ethical standards, social morality, people's world outlook, ideals, sentiments, consciousness, beliefs, sense of organization, and sense of discipline.

In practice, clearing up the universe will solve a number of problems. It will improve human kindness and gentleness and help families to be in concord, contradictions to be reconciled, society to be harmonious, the world to be peaceful, and the future to be bright. With these six solutions, human beings may approach an ideal future.

- *Human kindness and gentleness.* Human attributes are the inherent qualities of human beings that are formed under certain social systems and certain historic conditions. Human attributes, as the term suggests, refer to characteristics that only human beings possess. These kinds of characteristics distinguish human beings from any other living things (including animals and plants). For example, human attributes include the ability to use languages, written words, music, or other tools to communicate with each other; the ability to think deeply and to come to understand complicated concepts independently; the ability to create things; the ability to unite and coordinate with each other; the ability to handle immediate concerns and develop long-term strategies; and the ability to understand the objective world and to transform objective things. Other animals and plants do not possess these attributes. If both human beings and animals can possess a certain attribute, we can categorize it as an attribute of animals. These include the ability to reproduce, the ability to search for food, the ability to fear, and the ability to tend to favorable things and avoid harm. In other words, if a certain attribute is not possessed only by human beings, this attribute is not an attribute of human beings. Human beings evolved from animals, so the attributes of human beings are based on the attributes of animals. But human attributes are at a higher level and are possessed only by human beings. To be *kind and gentle* means to be mild and genial.

- *Families in concord.* When family members are in concord they are living together in a harmonious and friendly way.

A family is composed of people bonded with blood or marriage. These people live under the same roof with common budgets and expenses. Of course, this is just a theoretical concept. In reality, family life is closely related to the surrounding social life and affected by the current economy, politics, culture, and people's psychology and beliefs. No matter how independent a family looks, it more or less reflects the whole social phenomenon. Conversely, the so called "big world," namely social life, necessarily encompasses the characteristics of interpersonal relationships within a family, such as husband-and-wife and father-and-son relationships.

Everyone desires harmony in the family. The basis for a harmonious family lies in reasonable division of tasks and responsibilities, mutual respect, trust, and understanding. Only true common views can lead to healthy harmony.

- *Contradictions reconciled.* In dialectics, a contradictory relationship refers to a mutually dependent and repulsive relationship between various opposites in objects and human thoughts. In formal logic, it refers to the relationship of two concepts that repel each other or the relationship of two judgments that cannot both be true or false. In general, it refers to opposite objects repelling each other. Nowadays, in legal terms, reconciliation refers to a situation in which litigants agree to mutually give in so as to terminate a dispute or prevent further disputes without a court's involvement. Tolerance and lenience lead to dispute settlement. Both sides become friendly again. Sun Zi, a master of war in ancient China, said, "The supreme art of war is not to win all the wars, but to subdue the enemy without a war." This means that to win 100 percent of wars is not the best approach. Rather, getting the enemy to surrender without a war is the most brilliant way to win wars.

- *Harmonious society.* A harmonious society is an ideal that the human beings have been constantly and diligently pursuing. Philosophers in China and other countries have had many ideas about harmonious societies. A harmonious society should include democracy, rule of law, fairness, justice, honesty, friendship, vigor and vitality, stability, good social orders and Harmony between human beings and nature.

To have democracy and rule by law means that democracy is brought into full play, the basic strategy of ruling the country by law is truly implemented, positive factors in all fields are widely mobilized. Fairness and justice mean that the relationships between the interests of various parties in society are properly coordinated. In a harmonious society, social fairness and justice are truly safeguarded and realized. Honesty and friendship mean that all people in the society help each other, are honest, and keep promises. All people are equal and friendly when they are living in Harmony. Being full of vigor and vitality refers to the ability to respect all creative wishes favorable to social progress, support all creative activities, bring creative talents into play, and affirm the fruits of creation. Stability and good social order refers to social organizational mechanisms that are perfect. Social management is perfect. Social orders are good. The masses of the people live and work in peace and contentment. The society maintains stability and solidarity. Human beings and nature remain harmonious. Production develops well. The people lead rich lives and the ecology is healthy.

The above-mentioned basic features are interrelated and interactive. To construct a harmonious society, we must be human-oriented. We must continuously satisfy people's increasing daily material and cultural needs based on economic development, promote people's overall development, respect people's creative spirit, mobilize all active factors, and stimulate society's creative vitalities. We must stress social fairness, correctly reflect and take into consideration the interests of the masses in various fields, correctly handle people's internal and social conflicts, and properly coordinate relationships among various parties. Social harmony is not a harmony without differences. Constructing social harmony is both a goal and a process. We can gradually realize social harmony only through long-term hard work and continuous efforts.

- *World peace.* In a harmonious society, lasting peace would prevail in the world. Although the trend of world development is moving toward world peace, wars still exist in some places. Most of them were caused by ethnic conflicts and political disputes. For example, wars still exist in the Middle East in Israel and Palestine. There are also wars between the United States and certain Iraqi political groups. If we can settle conflicts among ethnic groups smoothly, we can reach common political viewpoints and avoid using force to solve problems; lasting world peace would not be far away. We must strengthen exchanges and blending among ethnic groups in the world, in order to increase good feelings among ethnic groups, reduce cultural differences, and realize understanding of religious beliefs. We must use reasonable diplomatic means to reach common political viewpoints. We must seek commonalities while reserving differences in order to avoid the use of arms to solve problems. Lasting world peace will be realized step by step as human society develops.

- *A bright future.* The future will be harmonious and fine. Human development will determine social development, while social development will directly affect human development. Only a highly developed and highly civilized society can enable everyone to realize the fullest and most complete development; only people who have realized complete development can better promote social development. And hence, the world will be a much better place. One tree cannot change the climate, but forests may change the climate. An individual cannot change society, but the joint efforts of the members of the entire society can change the society. We now want to construct a harmonious society. We need members of the entire society to make joint efforts. Only when people from high-level organizations to grassroots movements and social institutions along with every individual take concrete measures can a harmonious society be realized. Trickles form big rivers. The results of the efforts of various parts of society will become the development of society as a whole.

Everyone's efforts and everyone's development may promote social development. Social development can, in turn, create conditions for everyone's development. When the economy has developed, everyone may receive quality education. Everyone's talents may be brought into full play, and everyone's undertakings may achieve the most all-around development. Only when society has developed can people enjoy a better future. Harmony among people means that calmness and enthusiasm coexist. Firmness and the gentleness supplement each other. Virtue and the mighty force exist at the same time. People are healthy both physically and spiritually and are full of vigor and vitality. Harmony of society means that all members of society progress together. Various regions and various sectors develop at the same time, and every undertaking achieves sustainable development. People and society are all harmonious. Society and people make developmental strides together. Human development and social development are mutually constrained and mutually promoted.

To construct a harmonious society is to create the most favorable conditions for everyone's development. Every social member's efforts and development are contributions to the construction of a harmonious society. This is true for people's development and for social development. This is also true for harmony among people and the harmony of society. A society needs harmony, and so do a nation, a region, and an individual. Small-scale harmonies form a large-scale harmony, while a large-scale harmony promotes small-scale harmonies. Harmony is the unity of contradictions. Harmony is balance. Only when we are harmonious can we be full of vigor and vitality. Only when we are harmonious can we achieve sustainable development. So long as the members of society make joint efforts, continuously eliminating inharmonious factors and creating harmonious attributes, we will realize a harmonious society in due time. Harmony is human beings' further understanding of themselves, society, and nature. Mutual communications are also a component of harmony. So long as people seek major commonalities while reserving minor differences and seek minor commonalities while reserving major differences, humankind will definitely realize its bright future.

The Concept and Characteristics of the Culture of Harmony

The Culture of Harmony is a culture in which harmony is the ideological intention and culture is the manifesting form of that intention. It integrates ideological concepts, ideals, beliefs, social moralities, behavioral norms, and value orientations and contains the overall understanding and evaluation of the harmonious world. The Culture of Harmony is an organic integration of social development and cultural construction. Its spiritual intention contains elements of history and the nature of tradition and combines characteristics of ethnic groups, the world as a whole, and both traditional and modern times.

The Culture of Harmony is human beings' blueprint of the ideal society, the essential intention of which is harmony and benevolence. The essential factors of the Culture of Harmony originated at the very beginning of human civilization and rooted in ancient Oriental philosophy and Western religions. The culture's system is constructed within modern civilization. As an old Chinese saying goes, "Man is born with good nature." Various cultures, including religions such as Oriental Confucianism, Taoism, Buddhism, and Islam and Western Catholicism and Christianity were formed at the early stage of human existence. Buddhist scriptures and Taoist philosophies—whether they are teachings of sages, opinions of persons of virtue, or theories on God or Buddha—all try to guide people to develop toward truth, goodness, or beauty. This is determined by the common nature of human beings and is also the basis of mutual dialogue, mutual attraction, and even mutual integration of the cultures of various ethnic groups. If humankind did not have common genes and if the cultures of various ethnic groups did not have in common a rational faculty, human beings would not be able to communicate, assimilate, and merge with each other. The Culture of Harmony has been carried in the genes of civilization, existing in the cultures of various ethnic groups throughout the world and has become the common culture of human society as a whole.

The core value of the Culture of Harmony is the ability to operate in one's own ideal space without violating others' interests. The

Culture of Harmony contains no mutual coercion and no mutual violation; it commands people's respect for each other, mutual cooperation, and the seeking of commonalities while reserving differences and achieving common development.

The philosophical ideal of the Culture of Harmony is to become a universal outlook, wherein the world's core values are based on the principle of "Harmony with differences"—embracing differences while living harmoniously. In other words, we hold that we have the heaven above us, the earth below us, and the people in the middle on the earth. Above us, we strive for harmony with the heavens. Below us, we strive to be harmonious with the earth. In the middle on the earth, we strive for harmony with other people. In a sentence, we advocate that the heavens and human beings should combine. The heavens and human beings must integrate and unite. The heavens and human beings must be harmonious. We should be kind to all things in heaven or on the earth, both living and nonliving. We should merge all human beings and all things in heaven and on the earth into one. Human beings and all things in the heaven or on the earth should respect each other, love each other, and enjoy life and prosperity together. Such a philosophical idea, as a matter of course, should become a content of the Culture of Harmony, which is now continuously developing and should also become the basis of the Culture of Harmony.

In the philosophical ideal of the Culture of Harmony, one must seek common points in differences and respect the existence of differences. The Culture of Harmony is a union of commonalities and differences. In other words, the Culture of Harmony constructs a background of different colors. This unified background includes cultural characteristics of different skin colors, different beliefs, different organizations, different collectives, different ethnic groups, and different countries.

The humanistic philosophy of the Culture of Harmony is equality, friendliness, and universal love. The Culture of Harmony regards human beings and all things as independent subjects who equally exist in the space of the universe. It venerates harmony with the heavens, with the earth, and among people and promotes the harmonious survival and prosperity of all things in the universe.

The Culture of Harmony is an advanced culture that has been universally venerated in both the Orient and in the West and has been passed on from generation to generation. This culture guarantees that ethnic groups will maintain a harmonious coexistence, society will develop harmoniously, and we'll achieve lasting word peace.

CHAPTER THREE

BLUE PRINTS ON THE
CULTURE OF HARMONY

The Culture of Harmony and Demands of the New Era

When the ancient Greek civilization initiates the enlightenment for human civilization, when human creative thinking elevates to logic capabilities, when logic capabilities become the motivator for human society to move toward scientific civilization, when human renaissance once again elevates enlightenment of civilization to its summit, the philosophy society must call for the Culture of Harmony to be the leading force and the new era must have Harmony as its dominant theme in order to awaken the human civilization.

The emergence of any kind of leading culture is a result of selection, acceptance, and inheritance through cultural comparison along the evolutionary course of civilization. It was a historical necessity. In the contemporary era, there are two important global issues—the integration of the global economy and the integration of economy and culture. The integration of global economy reflects the expansion of economic space and the increase of interdependence among regions. The integration of economy and culture illustrates the issue of cultural orientation and that of culture's mission in global economic development. These two issues require three fields to lead the call for global implementation of the Culture of Harmony.

First, the trend toward global development must lead us toward Harmony. Globalization is a course that will lead contemporary human social life to a space in which it has surpassed the boundaries of countries and regions, the obstacle of space, and systematic and cultural obstacles; sought coordination and cooperation; and promoted integration. The trend has an important influence on the Culture of Harmony, creating an even greater demand for its implementation. The Culture of Harmony will become humanity's common political pursuit and universal value. In turn, the Culture of Harmony will lead and promote the reform of the economic and political systems reform. Just as UNESCO emphasizes, the driving force for realizing development actually exists in the culture. Culture is the cradle of development and the mother of human civilization.

The second call for the Culture of Harmony must come from the highly developed fields of science and technology. Scientific and technological developments, especially our deepening understanding of outer space and the universe urges humanity toward critical self-examination and to promote the Culture of Harmony as the leading force. Humankind is now making comprehensive efforts with the firmest determination to disseminate the Culture of Harmony. People are turning the Culture of Harmony into a culture of humanity that is respected and widely inherited. Humankind is also turning the Culture of Harmony into a basis for spiritual guidance and for establishing rules of human behaviors—rules that promote friendliness, good relationships between ethnic groups, and an all-around Harmony in the development of the economy and society. At the same time humankind must comprehensively pursue a high degree of harmony between individuals and between people and nature. Furthermore humankind must realize the ultimate goal of the cultural development of human beings.

The third call for Harmony must come from the development of information technology. The information society has helped various countries form an international environment for nonmaterial, territorial integrity and has constructed network systems for world civilization dissemination. We may say that the evolution of information technology and the information society has sped up the dissemination of the Culture of Harmony and has also provided a guaranteed time and space in which humans can lead the movement toward the Culture of Harmony.

Development and Dissemination of the Culture of Harmony in the Contemporary Era

The current human culture, in a strict sense, is a process of culture evolving from ignorance and cruelty to civilization. Why do I say that? Because violence, terror, and slaughter still exist in the current world. Humanity moves from no-theory times to civilized, splendid times, establishing common values and a new civilization with this epoch-making philosophy of the Culture of Harmony. In a world with Harmony as the major theme of civilization, human will construct the Harmony of Union based on the epistemology of "different yet harmonious and harmony with differences" and the methodology of "seeking commonalities in differences and respect differences in commonalities." Observing the history of human civilization, we can make the following conclusions. First, the Culture of Harmony is an epoch-making philosophy, which has become the foundation and guidance of all social development. The equal development of everyone is the norm of social life. Although it originated in China, it determines the future of the whole world. We should use the power of Harmony to understand the history of human civilization, tackle with the crises in the past and present development, and establish the law, theme, and norm of human society. Second, the society is a world of culture. Culture is the life of society and culture determines development of civilization. The differences of historical times are in fact the differences of culture. Third, we should make the Culture of harmony a law, because it guarantees human's equal and free creativity and development; it develops and surpasses all of current democracy and equality; it ensures the authenticity of equal development. The law of democracy only applies to democratic countries, whereas the law of Harmony applies to the whole world. The old era dies during the growth of the new era. The era of the Culture of Harmony will come. This is an era with equality for all, elimination of ignorance, cruelty, violence, suppression, plundering, and wars, and awakening of civilization. In the supreme human civilization, there should exist no disputes among ethnic groups, no borders among countries, and no countries on the earth. Moreover, the ideal world is a realization of human "unions" with freedom, equality, universal love and kindness, and Harmony. This mission is significant and takes a long journey. The development and dissemination of the Culture of Harmony is a necessary route toward the grand ideal.

CORRECTING HUMAN PREJUDICES

A number of intentions are behind human prejudices. The first is biased power politics. Prejudices advocate the law of the jungle and invasive expansion. The second is biased consciousness in terms of the desire to promote one's own beliefs. Prejudices allow us to respect only our own religion, advocate extreme ideas in which we deem our own beliefs the only ones worthy of respect, and even stir up others to exclude people who don't adhere to their own religious beliefs. The third is biased backward ethnical customs, insisting on

that tl
integr

In orc
we mi

A

ossified thoughts and behavior. The ethnical customs and traditions formed by the customary culture are habits to social individuals, and are customs to social groups. The biased customs would, under certain conditions, form strong forces for fighting. Such forces would overcome thousands upon thousands of horses and soldiers, and would overcome imperial power and military power. Biased customs are fearful forces. Prejudices are the origins of violence, terror, fighting, and even war and slaughter. We must use as our core value, the concept of operating in one's ideal space while not violating others' interests to correct various prejudices and to create harmonious and friendly cultural ideas, customs, and lifestyles.

Forming Core Values

B

C

The idea of values is the most important spiritual pillar of any ethnic group or any nation and the core of any cultural structure. To a certain extent, cultural differences are essentially value differences because values form the most obvious characteristics manifested in various cultures. We must remember that fostering the Culture of Harmony means operating in one's ideal space while not violating others' interests; this idea must form the core value for all human beings.

Leading the Human Spiritual World

The d
of H₂
the fi
harm
T
huma

We must base our spiritual world on the principle that Harmony is supreme, and universal love is borderless. We must spread the beliefs that kindness to our neighbors, friendliness, and harmonious living are the paths to achieving prosperity together. We must make firm, complete efforts to disseminate the philosophy of the Culture of Harmony—to turn the Culture of Harmony into the culture of humanity, believed, respected, and passed on to the next generation.

C

H
b
l
c
a

V
c
o
o
s
v
t
a
(
T
T
w
B
e
a
n
e
f
b
u
V
t
c
c